D0900076

Leisure and Pleasure in the Eighteenth Century

By the same author

Journey by Stages
Leisure and Pleasure in the Nineteenth Century

LEISURE AND PLEASURE IN THE EIGHTEENTH CENTURY

by

STELLA MARGETSON

CASSELL · LONDON

OLIVEIRA MEMORIAL LIBRARY
1825 MAY STREET
BROWNSVILLE, TEXAS 78520

CASSELL & COMPANY LTD
35 Red Lion Square, London, WC1
Melbourne, Sydney, Toronto
Johannesburg, Auckland

© *Stella Margetson* 1970

All rights reserved. No part of this publication
may be reproduced, stored in a retrieval system,
or transmitted, in any form or by any means,
electronic, mechanical, photocopying, recording
or otherwise, without the prior permission of
Cassell and Company Ltd.

First published 1970

I.S.B.N. 0 304 93665 0

Printed in Great Britain by
Cox & Wyman Ltd
London, Fakenham and Reading
F. 870

With love to dear Marie

ACKNOWLEDGEMENTS

I would like to acknowledge the great debt I owe to the authors, editors and publishers of the works listed in the Bibliography at the end of this book.

The eighteenth century is a huge field of study and to acknowledge each author separately an impossible task. But the voluminous letters and diaries of the period, so patiently deciphered by their several editors, have been an invaluable source of material; and since the balance of the material is always more generous in the reminiscences of the upper and middle classes than the less articulate members of the community, I would especially like to thank the Agricultural Press (Country-wise Books) for allowing me to quote at some length from *The Diary of a Farmer's Wife*, edited by Susan Beedell.

I am grateful to the librarians and staff of the British Museum, the Victoria and Albert Museum, the Guildhall Library, the Westminster Public Libraries and the Fawcett Library for their unfailing assistance; and I would also like to thank Lord Lambton, Sir Edward Thompson, the National Trust, the National Gallery, the Courtauld Institute of Art and the Radio Times Hulton Picture Library for permission to use the illustrations I have chosen.

CONTENTS

LIST OF ILLUSTRATIONS

LIST OF ILLUSTRATIONS

1

THE QUEEN

and

THE DUCHESS

WHEN QUEEN ANNE, 'ill of the goute and in extream agony', was carried to her coronation in Westminster Abbey in April 1702, she had no idea that the century just beginning was to become the golden age of leisure and pleasure in England. Nor did she realize that the foundations of peace and prosperity for many years to come would be laid down by the events of her short reign—by Marlborough's great victories which destroyed the despotic power of Louis XIV of France and left the way open for British trading round the world, and by the gradual growth of the system of parliamentary government at home, which in spite of much corrupt practice, gave the English a freedom quite unknown to any of their continental neighbours and a favourable opportunity to develop their native genius through the civilizing, intellectual refinements of the aristocracy and the sturdy individuality of the common people.

1

It was true that the century opened with many religious and political conflicts still undecided between the High Churchmen, the Dissenters and the Jacobite supporters of Roman Catholicism, between the Whigs and the Tories and their interpretation of their allegiance to the Crown. But the theory of the divine right of kings, which had so bedevilled the constitution in the previous century, was no longer the subject of heated controversy, and a satisfactory compromise had been reached in 1688 when Dutch William and his wife Mary had been invited to ascend the throne, thus ensuring the Protestant succession and the utter defeat of James II's brutal attempt to impose Roman Catholicism on the country.

Much bitterness still existed between the antagonistic forces operating from the past on the surface of the time. The bloodstained circuit of Judge Jeffreys was still within living memory and the conflict of loyalty to the anointed king still raw in the minds of those who had supported or abandoned him. And besides this, William III was very unprepossessing—no one liked him or took pleasure in his society. His favourite occupation was war, his only amusement hunting; and he was 'not very nice in the Company hee kept,' according to Sarah Churchill, the future Duchess of Marlborough, 'for by his choice hee had for the most part men that one should think oneself very miserable to bee condemned often to bee shut up with.' Yet while he reigned and even more so when his sister-in-law succeeded him, the fundamental strength of the nation began to emerge from the great depths of good sense latent in the people and to gather pace as it flowed into the broad stream of toleration and harmony that was to mark the English way of life all through the eighteenth century.

William had been accepted rather grudgingly. Anne was popular. She had courage, a kindly nature and a good store of common sense. It was not her fault if she was dull and devoid of imagination. Her life had not been easy, either as a child at the dissolute Court of her uncle King Charles II, or as a young woman exposed to the intrigue and the treachery of her father's fanaticism. And although she never deviated from her firm adherence to the Protestant faith, her path was not much sweeter in the joint reign of her sister Mary and William of Orange. Mary was jealous. They quarrelled about money and about Anne's lodgings in the Cockpit at Whitehall. At one time her guard was taken away and Mary rudely demanded the dismissal of her Lady of the Bedchamber. But Anne could be obstinate like all the Stuarts, and she held her ground. If Mary would not let her live in Whitehall with Sarah Churchill in attendance, then she would live somewhere else as a private person. She did not care a fig what anyone thought or said about it; she would 'rather live on bread and water between four walls' with her chosen friend, than enjoy the honours due to her as a royal Princess—for her trust in Sarah and their long friendship amounting to a passionate adoration on Anne's side, was the one great pleasure of her life.

She had married Prince George of Denmark in 1683 when he was blond and not unhandsome, suffering thereafter the long and tragic series of births and miscarriages which wrecked her health and were of no avail, since her only son to survive, the pale and sickly Duke of Gloucester, died at the age of eleven two years before she ascended the throne. By then she was prematurely old at thirty-seven and fond of her stupid husband, in whom no one else could find a spark of entertainment or originality either when he was drunk or when he was sober. Shut away in Kensington or at Windsor, they played ombre and basset together, the Queen more often than not swathed in ugly bandages and unable to take the air except in her *chaise roulante* with two gentlemen walking beside the horses' heads. It was not surprising in the circumstances if Queen

Anne's Court lacked glamour and was sparsely attended by those who still remembered the amoral gaiety of the pleasure-loving society surrounding King Charles II. Attendance was a matter of duty, of place-hunting for remuneration and reward, not of entertainment.

It was not surprising either that the Queen relied on Sarah Churchill. Their friendship had begun during their childhood at the Court of King Charles. Sarah Jennings had everything that was wanting in Anne. She had beauty —glorious golden hair, blue eyes and a wonderful complexion; a quick brain and, even as a child, a very shrewd idea of her way about. She said what she thought, speaking the truth as she saw it with an alarming disregard for whether the truth was acceptable to her audience or not; and she had a will of her own. What she thought or said was always right in her own opinion and she talked so well, with such gaiety and wit that she was very convincing.

This, then, was the lively and fascinating young girl the Princess found so exhilarating when they acted together in John Crowne's masque *Calisto and the Chaste Nymph* in 1674, when Sarah was fourteen and Anne four years younger. Their attraction for each other was immediate. Anne was timid and silent; Sarah forthright and voluble. Without much supervision from their elders, they could withdraw into some unregarded corner of the Court and spend all their leisure together, discussing their friends and relations and discovering each other. Romantic friendships—or, as Sarah called them, 'pretty Entertainments and Romantick Amusements to help the time to pass away'—were then the fashion between girls in their teens; secret meetings, clandestine letters and notes expressing their ardent love for each other, an excitement in their hours of idleness. But Anne meant it when she wrote to Sarah: 'I hope you will do me the justice to beleeve that I will never change . . . I am ye same I ever was and ever

will be to ye to the last moment of my life.' She was pro-
foundly stirred by a deep and lasting affection that only
events in the distant future would disrupt.

Sarah responded warmly, if not with quite the same
single-minded devotion. For her it was different—she had
pleasure elsewhere. At the age of fifteen, she fell in love
with Colonel John Churchill, who was ten years her
senior and had already distinguished himself in battle.
He was wonderfully handsome, gloriously brave, generous
and strong, yet gentle and kind and never for a moment
insincere. Of course he had been involved before—with
the notorious Barbara Castlemaine, Duchess of Cleveland
—and of course his family, disapproving of Sarah's lack
of material wealth, wanted him to marry the rich and ugly
Catherine Sedley instead. It did not matter—and neither
did the explosive ups and downs of their three years' long
courtship. They were married secretly some time in 1678
and it was a love-match, a romance which lasted all their
lives, for each was passionately devoted to the other and
after Marlborough's death, Sarah's only consolation was
her pride in his memory.

Anne strove very hard not to be jealous of her friend's
happiness—complacency was sometimes a virtue in her.
And by this time the two young women were so close that
all ceremony had been dropped between them at Anne's
suggestion. 'One day she proposed to me,' Sarah wrote,
'that whenever I should happen to be absent from her we
might in all our letters write ourselves by feigned Names
such as would import nothing of Distinction and Rank
between us. Morley and Freeman were the Names her
Fancy hit upon; and she left me to chuse by which of them
I would be called. My frank, open Temper naturally led
me to pitch upon Freeman and so the Princess took the
other; and from this Time Mrs Morley and Mrs Freeman
began to converse as Equals, made so by Affection and
Friendship.'

There were times, none the less, when Mrs Morley's patience was stretched rather far if Mrs Freeman was absent for too long, enjoying the pleasures of life at St Albans with her husband and her growing family. 'I hope ye little corner of your heart that my Lord Churchill has left empty is mine,' she wrote plaintively, and again: 'I cannot live without you, and tho I wish you and Mr Freeman everything your own harts can desire, you must not think ... that it is reasonable for you to live out of the world so long as I am in it.' Fortunately Mrs Freeman, though she found it very tedious to be closeted with Mrs Morley where 'there could be no manner of conversation', only the interminable games of ombre and basset as a diversion, did not think it reasonable to stay away from the Court all the time; she thought Mrs Morley's tenderness for her would enhance her husband's reputation—which it did.

She was not ambitious for herself, only for him, since besides loving him with all the ardour of a young and passionate woman, she was aware of his great qualities and admired his undeviating loyalty to his country. She saw the glory of Anne, the glory of Marlborough and the glory of England as one shining star of great splendour that would illuminate the world for ever; and for quite a time the reality did not fall far below her expectations. The Queen, backed up by Godolphin and his ministry, willingly supported the war against France. Marlborough's genius as a commander and his skill as a diplomat changed the whole balance of power in Europe and shattered the image of the French King's invincibility, while at home Sarah used her influence, if not always with great tact, with a brilliance that could not be resisted or denied. She was Groom of the Stole with a golden key of office, Mistress of the Robes, Keeper of the Privy Purse and Ranger of Windsor Park—an artful idea this of Mrs Morley's, since a pleasant lodge in the Park went with the appointment, encouraging Mrs Freeman to take up her residence there when the Court was at the Castle and her 'poor unfortunate, faithfull Morley' laid up with one of her attacks or in bed, dosing herself with 'Spa water and that most naucetious of all remedies, Rubarb'.

Anne wrote at least once, sometimes twice a day to her friend. She basked in the sunshine of her approval and it was only later that the first shadows began to appear on the shining surface of the united face they put upon the world. Perhaps Mrs Freeman got tired of Mrs Morley's doglike devotion, of her continual importunities and her dread of being deserted by the only friend she knew she could trust. Perhaps Mrs Morley began to see how domineering Mrs Freeman had become. If it was not one thing, it was another. She was always arguing about something: usually about those horrid Whig Lords—Sunderland, Wharton, Somers, Halifax and Orford—who had combined to form the powerful Whig Junto and were, in Mrs Morley's humble opinion, a pack of wolves. Then there was Abigail Hill, a poor relation of Mrs Freeman's and by her recommendation a Woman of the Bedchamber: a very restful sort of person after Mrs Freeman herself and clever, too, in calming Mrs Morley's anxiety; and there was nice Mr Harley, a moderate Tory, who did not mind coming up the backstairs when Mrs Hill told him Mrs Freeman wasn't there. It was all very worrying—expecially as Mrs Morley only wanted to do what was best for everyone and did not like being torn first one way and then another. After all she was Queen of England and surely she had the right to decide some things for herself, even if it meant displeasing her greatest friend? Not that she really wanted to—she still loved Mrs Freeman very dearly and simply could not—or would not—understand why she made such a terrible fuss when she discovered that Abigail Hill had secretly married Mr Masham, not only with Mrs Morley's consent, but actually in her presence at Dr Arbuthnot's lodgings.

B

It was Sarah's first intimation that a viper was nestling in the Queen's bosom and from that moment she saw herself as the victim of a fearful conspiracy. She believed that the fate of England hung upon this small domestic matter, as indeed it did; for Abigail was the pawn of the Tory party and the Tories were determined to undermine Marlborough's conduct of the war. Sarah saw it all happening, and she never for a moment thought of concealing her displeasure and her fury; in fact, she lost no opportunity of telling the Queen exactly what she thought. No one and nothing could stop her from bombarding the wretched woman with 'reasonable argument'. Even Marlborough's coded letter after the battle of Oudenarde, begging that 'Mrs Freeman would see what she so frequently obsarves that 42 [the Queen] is not capable of being chang'd by reason, so that you shou'd be quiet til the times comes in which she must change', had no effect whatever. His Duchess could not be quiet. She had got her teeth into the quarrel and what had once been the Queen's only joy in life was now a torment. Even the death of Prince George of Denmark, when Sarah was 'resolved not to say the least wry word to displease her', failed to heal the wound for, as Sarah was conducting the grief-stricken Queen away from Kensington to St James's Palace, she noticed that Anne, who was leaning heavily on her arm, 'had the strength to bend down towards Mrs Masham like a sail and in passing by went some steps more than was necessary to be nearer her'.

Things could not go on like this. Sarah felt she had been shabbily treated and that the Queen was guilty of ingratitude. Her righteous wrath blazed in a great flame of accusation and invective. The Queen must be *made* to see how she had abused her faithful friend and what ruin she would bring upon her country if she submitted to the Tory machinations of Harley, St John and the poisonous

Masham. But the Queen was sullen and, at their last meeting in 1710 when Sarah sought an interview with her in a desperate attempt to justify herself, utterly maddening. As once she had reiterated *ad nauseam* her protestations of affection and dependence, now she repeated over and over again one set phrase coined from one of Sarah's letters: 'You desired no answer, and you shall have none.' Against this uncomprehending wall of obstinacy, even Sarah could fight no longer. Mrs Morley had repudiated Mrs Freeman for ever.

Marlborough himself when he came back to England, though he fell on his knees at the Queen's feet and pleaded with her, could not effect a reconciliation. The Queen demanded the return of Sarah's golden key of office within two days and when she got it the same night, gave it to the scheming Duchess of Somerset, while that 'decembling creature' Abigail was appointed Keeper of the Privy Purse. Godolphin was cruelly put out of office after much faithful service, Harley and St John elevated to the peerage as Earl of Oxford and Viscount Bolingbroke; and before long Anne felt strong enough to dismiss Marlborough himself, while Harley made a disadvantageous peace with France behind his back.

All the cloud-capped towers of England's greatness that Sarah had envisaged appeared to be dissolving into ruin. Dean Swift, having deserted the Whigs and gone over to the Tories in the hope of being rewarded with a bishopric, took immense pleasure in writing a virulent and damaging attack on Marlborough, accusing him of peculation and self-aggrandizement in a pamphlet called *The Conduct of the Allies*. Even Blenheim Palace, that great monument to Marlborough's achievements slowly taking shape in the midst of the former royal estate at Woodstock and presented to the Duke in happier times by a grateful Queen, was in jeopardy. There was no money forthcoming from the Treasury to pay the stonemasons or the architect and by 1711 all work on the site was abandoned indefinitely. A few months later when England became altogether too unhealthy for the Duke and Duchess, they went abroad, leaving two men in charge of the unfinished mansion and its 200 acres of park and garden—Tilleman Bobart and Henry Joynes, who did absolutely nothing except fish in the lake for their own amusement.

Building was not resumed until the Duke and Duchess returned to England in triumph after the death of Queen Anne in 1714. But the Duchess had never really cared for Blenheim. She hated size and grandeur and much preferred Holywell, her modest country house near St Albans, or the house Wren built for her in Pall Mall. She had neither the imagination nor the aesthetic sensibility to appreciate Vanbrugh's heroic design and her 'indifferency' worried the Duke. 'I hope you will like it,' he wrote apropos of changing the style of the portico, 'for I should be glad we were always of one mind . . . for I am never so happy as when I think you are kind.' She did not like it much—or Vanbrugh's 'ridiculous bridge in the air, leading from nowhere to nowhere with next to no water underneath it'. With her practical nature, she thought it was time he got a roof on the building and made their private apartments fit for habitation, instead of occupying himself with the triumphal approach to a great useless pile of stone that was still not ready to be lived in, though more than £260,000 of public money had been spent on it or was still owing to the contractors.

Of course, the Duchess told Vanbrugh exactly what she thought, as she had told the Queen; for years she had been on the brink of quarrelling with him. But in taking a high and haughty line with this 'most sweet-natured gentleman', she made a grave mistake. Proud as he was of his conception of the great palace he was building for a great man, there came a time after the Duke's first serious illness, when he would take no more bullying from the Duchess. Her interference was insufferable; and though Vanbrugh kept his head and his good temper for months on end out of loyalty and respect for the Duke, he could bear it no longer when she wrote him one of her long letters running into many pages 'full of Far fetch'd Labour'd Accusations, Mistaken Facts, Wrong Inferences, Groundless Jealousies and strained Constructions'. Politely and with great panache, he told her to go to the devil. 'You have your end, Madam,' he wrote, 'for I will never trouble you more unless the Duke of Marlborough recovers so far [as] to shelter me from such intolerable Treatment.'

Vanbrugh was upset, but not—like the Queen— devastated. Few men ever took more pleasure from life. Even his early experience of eighteen months in various French prisons after he had been caught sketching the fortifications at Calais had done nothing to embitter his good nature. He made friends with his gaolers, dined well and drank burgundy with them, could speak French fluently and was extremely amusing and attractive. If the Bastille was not exactly the gayest place in the world for a young man to kick his heels, at least he made the most of his enforced leisure by studying its massive architecture and when he got bored with playing cards, writing a comedy in the style of the great Restoration dramatists, Wycherley and Congreve. Then suddenly, in 1692, he obtained his release and returned to England to become a Captain of Marines at £180 a year.

It was not very much for living a gay life in London, especially as Captain Vanbrugh enjoyed going out and about among the richest lords of the English aristocracy, who besides being so involved in politics, were patrons of the arts and the theatre. Indeed, it was they, as the cream of the audience, who had made the English theatre after the Restoration second to none in Europe and to them that the dramatists, actors, scene-painters and everyone connected with the stage looked for support. Squabbles were always going on between Christopher Rich, the Machiavellian patentee of Drury Lane, and the actors led by Thomas Betterton, now a veteran but still the undisputed master of the stage; and recently Betterton's company with the Lord Chamberlain's permission had gone over to the theatre in Lincoln's Inn Fields, leaving Drury Lane almost denuded of plays and players. Colley Cibber, then only twenty-five, managed to fill the void for a time both as actor and dramatist with his play *Love's Last Shift* and himself in the part of a fop called Sir Novelty Fashion; but a new dramatist was urgently needed, and when Vanbrugh suggested a sequel might be written, even the devious Christopher Rich was interested. Without more ado and very quickly Vanbrugh wrote *The Relapse, or Virtue in Danger,* which was staged in 1696 with Cibber as Lord Foppington. At the end of the first act the audience showed their pleasure in the comedy by a spontaneous outburst of applause and when the curtain fell, 'the force of its agreeable wit' had quite carried them away.

Vanbrugh's success, repeated a year later when *The Provok'd Wife* was put on by Betterton's company, gave him the entrée he was looking for into the intellectual and aristocratic society that ruled the taste of the town; his charm and his agreeable nature did the rest. Very soon he was elected a member of the exclusive Kit-Cat Club, which derived its odd name from the delectable mutton-pies served by a Quaker pastrycook named Christopher Cat, who kept a tavern near Temple Bar where the members were in the habit of meeting. Later he moved to a bigger tavern in the Strand, where:

> High o'er the gate he hung his waving sign,
> A Fountain Red with ever-flowing wine;

and here his famous pies, 'filled in with fine Eatable Varieties fit for Gods or Poets', were baked in dishes lined with sheets of paper covered in the many squibs, epigrams and eulogies which had been written about him.

Equally odd was the conjunction of the two founders of the Club, Lord Somers and Jacob Tonson, the publisher. Both were self-made men, but Lord Somers had hoisted himself into a powerful position as Lord Chancellor in King William's reign and as leader of the Whig Junto in Queen Anne's, whereas Jacob Tonson was a mere commoner with a shop in Chancery Lane. That the one did not condescend to the other was perhaps due to Tonson's extraordinary personality and the prestige he had acquired as the publisher of Dryden, Congreve and every other notable author of his time. He looked like a bull-frog— big-eared, fat-chopped and double-chinned; yet although he could be cunning and relentless, he was a good friend to those who discovered the genial side of his character and enjoyed his convivial company at the Kit-Cat meetings in London or at Barn Elms, his villa near Putney. 'The Kit-Cat wants you much more than you can want them,' Vanbrugh declared when the publisher-bookseller was away in Amsterdam. 'Those who remain in towne are in great desire of waiting on you at Barne-Elmes. . . . There will be a hundred thousand apricocks ripe in ten days; they are now fairer and forwarder than what I saw on the Queen's table at Windsor on Sunday—and such strawberries as were never tasted: currants red as blood too; and gooseberrys, peaches, pairs, apples, and plumbs, to gripe the gutts of a nation.'

Vanbrugh thought it was 'the best Club that ever met'. Its forty-eight members included the most intelligent and active Whig lords and some of the most brilliant writers of the day—Congreve, Addison, Steele and Arthur Maynwaring—besides Dr Garth, the celebrated physician, and Sir Godfrey Kneller, who painted all their portraits.

The talk was gay and witty and sometimes profound, the wine excellent, and the habit of toasting some lovely young woman to be the reigning queen of the year, then writing her name with a diamond on a drinking-glass, a charming tribute to the fair sex. When the Duke of Kingston brought his precocious and pretty little eight-year-old daughter, Lady Mary Pierrepont, to a meeting, she was feasted with sweetmeats and overwhelmed with caresses, while hearing her wit and beauty extolled on all sides. 'Pleasure,' she wrote afterwards, 'was too poor a word to express my sensations; they amounted to ecstasy.'

Meanwhile, Vanbrugh's active delight in the society of the Kit-Cats helped to decide his future, for it was his friendship with Charles Howard, 3rd Earl of Carlisle, that first encouraged him to turn his thoughts towards architecture. Carlisle was young and rich, 'a gentlemen of great interest in the country and very zealous for its welfare', and he was anxious to replace the ancient castle he had inherited from his ancestors in Yorkshire with the most fashionable and splendid mansion a modern architect could conceive. He might have commissioned the Surveyor of the Works, Sir Christopher Wren, or his Deputy William Talman; he wanted the best available talent and at the same time to imitate the opulence of the Baroque ideal he had seen translated into stone on his continental travels. Wren's individual style was perhaps not showy enough to please his taste. Vanbrugh had no single building to his credit and apparently no experience; but he had ideas and enthusiasm and his astonishing facility for roughing out plans and elevations was persuasive. Carlisle took him off to Yorkshire and the foundation stone of Castle Howard was laid in the spring of 1701.

The architect and the Earl—unlike the architect and the Duchess later on—were in complete accord from the very beginning, and with Hawksmoor as Vanbrugh's technical assistant, the major part of the great house was erected in less than five years. Nothing like it had ever been seen in England before. The superb feeling for mass and outline with the bold ornamentation of towers, domes and pinnacles in relation to the high central cupola proclaimed the genius of the architect, working on a dramatic scale that had never been thought of for a private mansion. And in spite of the height and the immensity of the interior, Vanbrugh wrote: 'I am much pleased here (amongst other things) to find Lord Carlisle so thoroughly convinced of the Conveniencys of his new house, now he has had a years tryall of it. And I am the more pleased with it, because I have now a proof that the Duchess of Marlborough must find the same conveniency at Blenheim. For my Lord Carlisle was pretty much under the same Apprehensions with her, about long Passages, High Rooms etc. But he finds what I told him to be true. That those Passages would be so far from gathering and drawing wind as he feared, that a Candle wou'd not flare in them. Of this he has lately had the proof, by bitter stormy nights in which not one Candle wanted to be put in a Lanthorn. . . . He likewise finds, that all his Rooms, with moderate fires Are Ovens.'

If the Duchess of Marlborough was not convinced by Lord Carlisle's experience, he, at least, was always a grateful friend and patron. Through him Vanbrugh was appointed Comptroller of the Works in place of Talman and, with Wren and Hawksmoor, worked on the rebuilding of Greenwich; and when he was later dismissed by Queen Anne for his loyalty to Marlborough, it was to Castle Howard that he went for consolation. Here he found pleasant company and 'very good housekeeping' and his faith in himself was restored by walking about the grounds with his noble friend, discussing the improvements they could make with a temple here or a statue there to set off the grandeur of the park. His natural ebullience and his sense of humour were proof against the disappointments he suffered. 'I am not one of those who drop their Spirits on every Rebuff,' he wrote cheerfully. 'If I had, I had been underground long ago!' And that same little girl who had been toasted by the Kit-Cats, now married to Edward Wortley Montagu, wrote a malicious and amusing account of his stay in Yorkshire. 'I can't forbear entertaining you with our York lovers,' she told her friend. 'Strange monsters you'll think, love being as much forced up here as melons. In the first form of these creatures, is even Mr Vanbrugh. Heaven, no doubt, compassionating our dullness has inspired him with a passion that makes us all ready to die with laughing; 'tis credibly reported that he is endeavouring at the honourable state of matrimony, and vows to lead a sinful life no more. . . . Tis certain he keeps Monday and Thursday market (assembly day) constantly . . . but you know Van's taste was always odd; his inclination to ruins has given him a fancy for Mrs Yarborough: he sighs and ogles so, that it would do your heart good to see him; and she is not a little pleased, in so small a proportion of men amongst such a number of women, that a whole man should fall to her share.'

Lady Mary, as she so often did, was exercising her wit at the expense of the truth, for Vanbrugh had no intention of tying himself up with an old woman. Indeed, he surprised everyone—and himself too, perhaps—by asking Colonel Yarborough of Heslington Hall for the hand of his lovely young daughter Henrietta. She was twenty-five and her father at fifty-four the same age as his prospective son-in-law. It was not easy for Vanbrugh to break the news to his friends. 'There has now fallen a Snow up to ones Neck. . . . In short, 'tis so bloody Cold, I have almost a mind to Marry to keep myself warm,' he wrote to the Duke of Newcastle a few days before the wedding; and then to Jacob Tonson, that inveterate bachelor: 'I

have taken this great Leap in the Dark, Marriage. . . .
Don't be too much dismay'd however, for if there is any
truth in Married Man (who I own I ever esteem'd a very
lying creature) I have not yet repented. Thus far you may
believe me; if I offer more, 'tis like you won't; so I have
done.'

Far from ever repenting, Vanbrugh found an immeasur-
able increase of happiness in his young wife and the son
that was born to them at a time when the world was again
treating him very harshly. He had plenty of commissions
—Seaton Delaval for the 'mad Admiral', Eastbury in
Dorset for the equally eccentric and very rich Bubb
Dodington, Grimsthorpe Castle and Nottingham Castle;
but the post of Surveyor to the Works, which he had once
refused out of respect and affection for the ageing
Christopher Wren, was given to a nonentity when Wren
finally retired, and the Duchess of Marlborough, after the
death of the Duke, still went on ragging him like a dog
with a bone. The Duke left over £2,000,000, yet the
Duchess went to court to prevent Vanbrugh obtaining the
£1,663 he claimed was due to him for his unfinished work
at Blenheim, and it was only when the architect appealed
directly to another of the Kit-Cats, Sir Robert Walpole,
that he got his money 'in Spight of the Huzzys teeth'.

He did not live long to enjoy his triumph. A year later
he died after a short illness, his attractive and affectionate
personality sadly missed by his wife and his friends and
even by his one and only enemy. For the Duchess of
Marlborough was ageing and indeed lived until she was
eighty-four with no pleasure left in life except in quarrelling.
When the arrogant Duke of Somerset lost his wife and
begged her to marry him, she replied: 'If I were young
and handsome as I was, instead of old and faded as I am,
and you could lay the empire of the world at my feet, you
should never share the heart and the hand that once
belonged to John, Duke of Marlborough.' And no one

ARNULFO L OLIVEIRA MEMORIAL LIBRARY
1825 MAY STREET
BROWNSVILLE, TEXAS 78520

else, not even her family, could share her heart any longer. She quarrelled with her daughters and their husbands and went on quarrelling with her grandchildren. Yet, 'she had still at a great age considerable remains of beauty', according to Lady Mary Wortley Montagu, 'most expressive eyes and the finest hair imaginable, the colour of which she said she had preserved unchanged by constant use of honey-water.'

If only the Duchess had imbibed a little honey-water instead of rinsing her hair in it, she might not have found herself so alone and unloved in her old age. As it was she was still full of energy and spent her time in the house overlooking St James's Park that Wren had designed for her, for ever writing and rewriting her memoirs in a final attempt to justify herself and her lord. It was not even certain whether she believed in a reunion after death with her beloved Duke; what concerned her more was the disposal of his diamond-studded sword, for 'I do think Lady Bateman is capable of getting it to make buckles for stays' she wrote in despair of her granddaughter's irresponsibility. Life, it seems, had taught her to trust no one and pleasure had long since vanished in the years when she was young and sure of getting her own way. 'I am packing up to be gone', she wrote to Francis Godolphin in 1744 and two months later she was dead, leaving behind none to mourn her, only the memory of her irascible temper and her astonishing vitality.

2
FOPS
and
FASHION

FASHIONABLE LIFE IN London was centred in and about St James's Street and Pall Mall, not far from the Duchess of Marlborough's house. Here were the chocolate houses, White's and the Cocoa-Tree, patronized by the Tories; Ozinda's, another haunt of theirs, and the St James's Coffee House, where the Whigs forgathered. A Tory would not be seen at the St James's any more than a Whig would go to Ozinda's or to White's, though politics were not the only concern of the man of fashion. Gambling, gossip and the latest mode in wigs and waistcoats were equally important; wining and dining and going to the play filled the dizzy round of his days and nights. The fops, the wits and the beaux of society were frivolous, idle and extravagant, and vicious, too: quick to draw their swords and if they had courage enough, to settle their disputes at dawn in Hyde Park, apt to seduce a woman and leave her lying in the gutter, or to fondle their young footmen with undisguised affection. They took their leisure for granted and snatched at their pleasures with greedy fingers. 'Creatures compounded of a Perriwig and a Coat laden with Powder as white as a Miller's, a face besmear'd with Snuff, and a few affected airs,' one observant traveller from France noted. 'All the more remarkable in England, because generally speaking the English Men dress in a plain uniform manner.'

Dressing well was expensive. A smart, full-bottomed periwig made of female hair cost anything up to £300 and not to have it in perfect curl was to commit an outrage against the tyranny of fashion. Fortunately, anyone could buy a shilling bottle of 'Secret White Water' at the Glover's Shop under the Castle Tavern in Fleet Street which, it was claimed, 'being used over Night, according to Directions, performs a Curl by next Morning as substantial and durable as that of a new Wig, without damaging the Beauty of the Hair one jot.' But the true fop sent to France for his curiously embellished ivory and tortoiseshell combs and was in the habit of combing his wig in public when sitting in the side-box at the playhouse or visiting ladies in their drawing-rooms. The ornamentation of his person took him hours in the morning and kept him busy all day. His gold or silver snuff-box had a mirror in the lid that reflected the condition of his make-up every time he took a pinch of snuff, and he was constantly titivating his appearance as the heat of the wax candles burning at night melted his rouge away and the exhausting labour of amusing himself wore down his resistance.

To deck himself out in the finest clothes money could buy was his main preoccupation. Notice of a robbery from a gentleman's house in London showed the extent of one fashionable wardrobe, for among the garments stolen were: 'a Dove Coloured Cloth Suit embroider'd with Silver, and a pair of Silk Stockings of the same

Colour; a Grey Cloth Suit with Gold Buttons and Holes; a Silk Drugget Salmon Coloured Suit lin'd with white Silk; a flower'd Satin Nightgown, lin'd with a Pink coloured Lustring, and a Cap and Slippers of the same; a yellow Damask Nightgown lin'd with Blue Persian and a Scarlet Silk net Sash to tye a Nightgown.' Evidently this was a gentleman who took his smartness to bed with him, though he would have worn his elegant nightgown, or dressing-gown, with cap and slippers to match at his morning levee when curious visitors, eager to discover his secrets, called to watch his lengthy *toilette*.

He was lucky not to lose his shirts as well. Even Swift, who was not extravagant in his dress, sent to Holland for his shirts and paid a lot for them, though he was not frivolous enough to display his linen by leaving his waistcoat unbuttoned. This was said to have 'a most killing effect on the fair sex', one writer remarking that 'a sincere heart has not made half so many conquests as an open waistcoat'. A good leg likewise added to the modish fop's attractions. Apart from being able to buy padding for his calves if they were skinny, he spent a fortune on his immaculate silk stockings and buckled shoes with high red heels and took care never to walk anywhere in the wet if he could avoid it, but to be carried in a sedan-chair from one evening engagement to another. He might have his own private sedan lined with crimson velvet and trimmed outside with gold and silver ornaments, or he could hire a chair for 1s a mile. Either way he was liable to be 'shaken up in much disorder', for the public chairmen were a quarrelsome, rascally set of roughs all too fond of the bottle and the private footmen were not much better. They were supposed to observe certain rules in the streets:

Yet who the Footman's Arrogance can quell
Whose Flambeau gilds the Sashes of Pell Mell,

Gay asked, and it was not uncommon for the liveried servants of the rich to start a brawl with the public chairmen, especially as they claimed precedence for their lordly occupants.

Ladies, too, found the sedan-chair convenient and better than travelling by coach, since the chairmen carried them right inside the front door and deposited them in dirty weather, dry and unbespattered by the foul mud of the streets. Visiting was one of their chief amusements, playing at cards and talking scandal over a dish of tea their most constant delight. For if the gentlemen took their leisure for granted, the ladies hardly knew what to do with their idleness. 'I lie in Bed till Noon,' one of them declared, 'dress all the Afternoon, Dine in the Evening and play at Cards till Midnight; read lewd Plays and winning Romances; love my Page, my Monkey and my Lap Dog because they are foreign Creatures, and hate everything that Old England brings forth, except it be the temper of an English husband and the liberty of an English wife.'

There were plenty of young wives who were faithful to their husbands; but to play the flirt or to cuckold one's spouse if he happened to be old and rich, was all part of the game in the gay world of sophisticated society. Painted, powdered and patched, and larded with perfume to dispel the unpleasant odours of not washing very often with anything so common as soap and water, the ladies dressed themselves in high fashion to excite the curiosity of the opposite sex, and their unerring instinct for pleasure was freely suggested. The most fetching of their gowns were cut low and worn over very tight stays, which were deliberately exposed—hence the Duchess of Marlborough's fear of Lady Bateman picking the diamonds out of her grandfather's sword to decorate her buckles and tags. The tucker or modesty piece, ostensibly used to conceal the bosom, was a little muslin frill set inside the dress, guaranteed to attract more glances than it repelled, and the apron a strange fancy of the feminine brain designed to express the bashful appeal of a chaste waiting-woman. Fine silks and brocades, 'silver Tishea, Pudsway Silks, Shaggs, Tabbeys, Mowhairs, Grazets, Brochés, Flowered Damasks, Flowered Lustrings, Silk Plushes and Farendines' were some of the rich materials the ladies could choose from, and they were displayed with great effect at the New Exchange in the Strand, which was the most elegant shopping centre of the *beau-monde*. Here, under the covered arcade with its separate counters, almost anything could be bought: gloves and ribbons, silk stockings, yards of gold and silver lace, rich fans, French tweezers, scissors, combs and baubles of all kinds; and here also, according to Ned Ward, the young shopgirls themselves were dangerously alluring and sometimes for sale, 'a living gallery of Beauties, whose pretty roguish ways' made him feel he had entered a seraglio.

Ward, a good-humoured wit, who kept a tavern near Gray's Inn and wrote *The London Spy* which appeared regularly every month, admired pretty women and despised the pretty fops who chased them round the town. He grew lyrical about the ladies of quality who walked in the Mall 'to refresh their charming Bodies with the Cooling and Salubrious Breezes of the Gilded Evening'. There never was a more pleasurable sight than this fashionable parade under the green avenue of trees leading to the long water of the canal. 'We could not possibly have chose a Luckier Minute to have seen the delightful Park in its greatest Glory and Perfection,' he declared, 'for the brightest Stars of the Creation sure were moving here with such awful State and Majesty that their Graceful Deportments bespoke 'em Goddesses.' But the men, he thought, were of quite a different calibre: 'It seemed to me as if the World were Turn'd Top-Side turvey, for the

c

ladies looked like undaunted Heroes, fit for Government or Battle, and the gentlemen like a parcel of Fawning,
Flattering Fops, that could bear Cuckledom with Patience,
make a Jest of an Affront and swear themselves very
faithful and humble Servants to the Petticoat . . . as if their
Education had been amongst Monkeys, who (as it is said)
in all cases given the Pre-eminence to their Females.'

With one eye on the entertainment of his readers and
the other fixed on his image of the blunt and insular type
of Englishman he admired, Ward did his best to kill the
beau by ridicule, thereby assisting the new and more sober
trend in morals and manners soon to be followed by
other writers of greater distinction. 'A Beau is a Narcissus
that is fallen in Love with himself and his own Shadow,'
he wrote. 'Within Doors he is a great Friend to a great
Glass, before which he admires the Works of his Taylor
more than the whole Creation. His Body's but a Poor
Stuffing of a Rich Case, like Bran to a Lady's Pincussion.
. . . His Head is a Fool's Egg, which lies hid in a Nest of
Hair. His Brains are the Yolk, which Conceit has Addled.'

Yet London society was by no means made up of
noodles. Even the audiences at the Theatre Royal in
Drury Lane, where the fops in the side-boxes and the pit
were apt to make a great nuisance of themselves with their
silly chatter and their lascivious behaviour towards the
ladies on the stage and in the auditorium, were composed
to some extent of intelligent playgoers who took a real
interest in the drama; and the original failure of Vanbrugh's palatial new theatre in the Haymarket designed
for Betterton and his company was not due to the stupidity
of the audience or to the ineptitude of the actors, but to the
architect's misjudgement of the acoustics.

Thomas Betterton, though old, was still a great actor
with over forty years' experience on the stage; his two
leading ladies, Madam Barry and 'Matchless' Bracegirdle,
could still inspire their audience with delight in the

comedies of Congreve or command their passionate
attention in the bloodstained and awesome tragedies of
Dryden and Otway. By 1707, however, all three of them
were ready for retirement and a new combination of talent
rising from the young company at Drury Lane began to
dominate the theatrical scene. Colley Cibber was an
excellent administrator apart from his capabilities as a
character actor and a concoctor of plays. He took the
trouble to study 'the restless jealousy and fretful impatience' which kept his brother-actor, Robert Wilks,
'lean to his last hour' and when they fell out with each
other, resorted to humming an air to himself, 'a little out
of tune if the storm grew very high', as it often did. For
Wilks was vain and touchy, with an uncontrollable Irish
temper, but the idol of the public until Barton Booth
came forward to challenge his pre-eminence and the
rivalry between them kept Cibber humming more out of
tune than ever in his efforts to induce them to work
peacefully together. Wilks was brilliant in comedy; Booth
with his aristocratic air and melodious voice more successful in tragedy. Between them they inherited the mantle of
Betterton, while one highly versatile actress, Anne
Oldfield, combined in her own person the charming wit of
Mrs Bracegirdle and the tragic splendour of Madam Barry.

Anne Oldfield was discovered by the penniless and
disreputable Irish playwright, Captain Farquhar, serving
in the bar parlour at the Mitre Tavern in St James's
Market, her father, a trooper in the Horse Guards, having
left his widow and his little daughter nothing except his
hat with the tall white plumes, his scarlet coat and his
empty boots. She was lively, precocious and at the age of
fifteen, already very beautiful, with large, expressive eyes
set in an oval-shaped face and a tall, graceful figure with
long, slender legs. Having learnt to read, she had found
pleasure in getting the plays of Beaumont and Fletcher
by heart, speaking the parts out loud 'with so proper an

Emphasis and such agreeable Turns suitable to each Character' that Farquhar was astonished and delighted. None the less, when he recommended 'this jewel he had found by accident' to Vanbrugh, who got her into the company at Drury Lane, Cibber remained totally unimpressed by her abilities, and it was not until three years later when she took the part of Leonora in John Crowne's comedy *Sir Courtly Nice* that he had to admit his mistake. 'She had a just occasion to triumph over the error of my judgment, by the amazement that her unexpected performance awak'd me to,' he declared. 'So forward and sudden a step into nature I had never seen; and what made her performance more valuable, was, that I knew it all proceeded from her own understanding, untaught, and unassisted by any more experienc'd actor.'

The daughter of Trooper Oldfield was, in fact, extremely intelligent as well as extremely beautiful. She fascinated Arthur Maynwaring, who 'selected her from all the Fair Part of Creation to be his Bosom Companion and share his Joys and Cares', as much by her rare sensibility as by the loveliness of her face and figure. And this was no casual affair of pleasure between a distinguished member of the Kit-Cat Club and a woman of the theatre; they loved each other and lived as man and wife until Maynwaring's death nine years later. At their house in New Southampton Street, off the Strand, they shared their happiness and comfort with their small son, kept 'a good table with champagne and burgundy their favourite wines' and entertained their friends among 'the great, the gay and the fair'. Anne's natural charm, her style and her elegance silenced her most formidable critics among Maynwaring's family and gave her a leading position in society, which no other actress had yet achieved. Her clothes, her fans, the way she dressed her hair and wore the jewellery Maynwaring gave her, set the fashion and gave proof that she was no shameless huzzy, no raffish player of easy virtue, but a woman to be respected and admired. And she continued to work hard in the theatre, adding lustre to her reputation when she extended her range as an actress from comedy to tragedy. As Marcia in Addison's *Cato* she gave a superb performance, and she inspired Nicholas Rowe to write his 'she-tragedies' for her with a heroic woman instead of a man at the centre of the action—plays that were acceptable to the growing number of persons who believed 'the theatre should not be a licentious place to corrupt the minds of the people, but a school of manners and virtue'.

Indeed, the dissolute, amoral attitude towards life of the post-Restoration era was dying from a surfeit of indulgence and nowhere more quickly than in the theatre. Following on the puritanical outburst of Jeremy Collier, a non-juring clergyman, who had accused Congreve and Vanbrugh of obscenity, bawdiness and blasphemy in his *Short View of the Immorality and Prophaneness of the English Stage,* Queen Anne had issued several proclamations whereby 'all Stage Players, Mountebanks and all other Persons mounting Stages' were requested to submit their 'Several Plays, Drolls, Farces, Interludes, Dialogues, Prologues and other Entertainments' to her Master of the Revels at his office in Somerset House, 'to be perused, corrected and allow'd under his hand'. And this form of censorship was welcomed by Cibber, who remembered the days when ladies were 'decently afraid of venturing barefaced to a new comedy, till they had been assur'd they might do it without risque of an insult to their modesty'; or—rather worse in its consequences—'if their curiosity were too strong for their patience', came into the sideboxes and the pit wearing masks to conceal their identity, ladies of quality thus being indistinguishable from ladies of the town.

Such behaviour belonging to the dissipated, rakish generation that had thrived on the indecencies permitted in the theatre, was now deplored and a nicer, more refined attitude to their pleasure expected of both the audience and the actors. Through yet another proclamation, the Queen attempted to stop the gentlemen in the auditorium from going behind the scenes or climbing on to the stage to lark about with the actresses while the performance was going on. But this practice continued to appeal to the beaux who went to the playhouse to show themselves off and was described in Sir Richard Steele's account of one who, 'getting into one of the Side-boxes on the Stage, was disposed to show the whole Audience his Activity by leaping over the Spikes and passing from thence to one of the Entering Doors, where he took Snuff with a tolerable good Grace, display'd his fine Cloathes, made two or three feint Passes at the Curtain with his Cane, then faced about, affected to survey the whole House, bow'd and smiled at random and shew'd his Teeth, which were some of them indeed very White.'

No doubt the beau had reason to be vain about his teeth if some of them were 'indeed very White', considering that tooth-powder was made out of pulverized coral blended with Portugal Snuff and tooth-brushes out of the roots of marsh-mallow fried in a mixture of rectified spirits, dragon's blood and rose-water. Black teeth rotting at an early age were more general, hence the ladies having to laugh behind their fans; and dentistry was a very doubtful experiment carried out by barbers, apothecaries, tavern-keepers and quacks, who bought teeth from healthy country boys and girls willing to have them drawn for a few shillings and used them to make expensive and painful dentures for the upper classes. But apart from showing his teeth, the beau's conceit and his bad manners were deliberately offensive to the more serious playgoers at Drury Lane and equally so when he deserted the playhouse for the new Italian opera at the Queen's Theatre in the Haymarket. For suddenly the drama became a less fashionable form of diversion than the opera and the novelty of hearing famous singers brought over from Italy set the whole town talking.

Before the celebrated *castrato* Nicolini appeared for the first time in 1707 with Valentini and an Englishwoman, Mrs Tofts, 'singing in the Italian manner', opera in London had been a patchy affair with some of the performers singing in Italian and some in English and the music concocted from bits and pieces by separate composers. Now, thanks to the enthusiasm of the Duke of Manchester, who as Queen Anne's Ambassador to Venice had discovered how opera was performed in Italy, the best singers were engaged for the Haymarket and London went mad over them.

Nicolini, 'by pleasing the eye as well as the ear' was considered by some to be the greatest of all the *castrati* and to have excelled his even more highly paid successors, Senesino and Farinelli. His voice had 'a strong, clear sweetness that ravished his auditors' and according to Addison, his 'every limb and finger' contributed to the part he was acting, while 'there was scarce a beautiful posture which he did not plant himself in'. Catherine Tofts in matching herself up to so great a foreign artist, showed extraordinary self-confidence. But 'the beauty of her fine proportioned figure and the exquisitely sweet silver tone of her voice, with that peculiar, rapid swiftness of her throat, were perfections not to be imitated by art or labour'. And she knew the value of her charms. She demanded a salary of £500 for the season and an extra allowance for 'locks for hair, jewels, ribbons and muslins for vails etc', besides charging the admiring gentlemen who flocked round her, a guinea a time for each kiss they gave her. She did not, however, enjoy the pleasures of her success for very long. Soon after she married Joseph Smith, the British Consul in Venice, she became insane and spent the rest of her life hidden away in her husband's

vast *palazzo* on the Grand Canal, while he entertained the
visiting English lords and recommended them to buy the
paintings of his protégé, Canaletto. Occasionally she was
to be seen hovering about the garden, singing snatches
from the operas she had graced with so much spirit,
happily without realizing that her public had vanished
like a mirage on the lagoon.

In London she was quickly forgotten as the nobility
and the gentry crowded into the Queen's Theatre in the
spring of 1711 to hear a new opera called *Rinaldo* by a
brilliant young German, who had already succeeded in
Italy and was now on his first visit to England. Handel
intended to startle his new audience—and did; not only
by the dramatic colouring of the arias in *Rinaldo*, which
were superbly sung by Nicolini and Boschi, but also by the
excellence of his own direction of the performance from
the harpsichord. It was a new experience; nothing like it
had ever been heard in London before. Even the wits and
the beaux in the side-boxes stopped eating sweetmeats and
chattering among themselves to give their attention to the
stage and the young composer received an ovation.

He was twenty-six and Kapellmeister to the Elector of
Hanover, whose Court was far from exciting. It was not
surprising therefore, if his triumph at the Queen's Theatre
persuaded him to ask the Elector for leave to return to
England the following year and that, when he did return,
he made the most of being fêted by the young Earl of
Burlington at his mansion in Piccadilly and by the self-
made millionaire Duke of Chandos, who maintained a
private orchestra of thirty-three professional musicians
in his opulent palace at Edgware. For a time he lived with
'Princely Chandos' at Cannons, where 'his mornings were
employed in study, and at dinner he sat down with men
of the first eminence for genius and abilities'; and through
Lord Burlington's mother, he came into favour at the
English Court, poor Queen Anne, weary of life and the

vexations of Whig and Tory politics, being rather pleased
to have captured him from the hateful Hanoverian Prince
she knew was destined to succeed her.

What Handel himself had not reckoned with in his
delight at being so handsomely entertained in England,
was the Elector's displeasure at his long absence from
Hanover; and things might have gone very ill with him
when the Elector was called to the English throne in 1714
if the new King had not been genuinely moved by his
music. Whether or not the legend is true that George I
forgave him after being serenaded from a neighbouring
barge during a water party on the Thames by the dulcet
harmony of the young composer's *Water Music,* he
certainly behaved with unusual generosity, confirming the
pension of £200 a year that Handel had received from
Queen Anne and adding another £200 to it. In his
perplexity at the ways of the English which were so
foreign to his Germanic upbringing, and in a strange
country where he could not even speak the language or
understand what anyone was saying, perhaps the new
King took more pleasure in encouraging the genius of his
compatriot than in any other of the doubtful privileges
which had been thrust upon him by his accession to the
throne. The English aristocracy found him and his fat
mistresses disagreeable and dull and did not bother to
conceal their feelings; yet his patronage of the opera and
of the public concerts which Handel arranged, created a
new standard of musical appreciation in London and
without his financial support, the first Royal Academy of
Music, founded in 1719, would not have prospered.

At the King's Theatre, or the Royal Italian Opera
House as it was now called, Handel's only rival in popularity was Bononcini, a suave and successful Italian
composer, whose opera *Astarto* was wildly acclaimed and
split the musical public into factions, one side opting for
Handel and the other for Bononcini. Neither composer

suffered much from this feud, since it generated an extra interest in both, just as the rivalry between the two *prima donne*, Cuzzoni and Faustina, engaged for the season in 1725, added fire and fury to the operatic stage, stimulating their divided supporters to frantic outbursts of feeling. Cuzzoni had arrived first in 1722; and the second harpsichord-player at the opera, Sandoni, having been sent to Dover to meet her, promptly married her *en route* for London, perhaps attracted more by the fabulous salary of £2,000 that she demanded for the season than by her other fascinations, for she was dumpy and rather plain and her difficult temperament was notorious. Handel had written *Ottone* for her début, and he took a very strong line with her, threatening to throw her out of the window when she refused to sing one of the arias in it, proving by the success she eventually achieved, that he was absolutely right in his judgement. Cuzzoni and *Ottone* took the public by storm. Half-guinea tickets for the second performance were offered at black-market prices in the fashionable coffee houses and the Haymarket was crammed with coaches, sedans and hackney carriages setting down their passengers, who then had to fight their way into the theatre to await the appearance of their idol.

The following season she sang with Senesino in *Giulio Cesare* and again in *Rodelinda,* wearing a diaphanous, brown silk gown trimmed with silver, which shocked some of the ladies and delighted most of the gentlemen in the audience, though all were agreed that her voice was miraculous. Then Faustina arrived at a salary of £2,500 and Handel was posed with the problem of giving the two *prima donne* an equal number of arias of precisely equal importance in his new opera *Alessandro*. Both ladies were in love with the hero, played by Senesino, both had a duet with him and exactly the same number of arias, but even Handel could only arrange for one of them to marry him before the final curtain. Cuzzoni was the more tender and lyrical of the two, Faustina more brilliant and powerful and a better actress; and while the contrast between them gave their duets together a highly dramatic significance on the stage, it also excited a violent partisanship among their fashionable audience, which inflamed their egotism and played upon their nerves. Their first season together was harmonious enough to all appearances, but at the end of their second, urged on by the frenzied applause, cat-calls and boos of their divided followers, they actually came to blows 'in the most horrible and bloody battle' during a performance of *Astianate* in the presence of the Princess Caroline.

The reputation of the Italian Opera House was not improved by this unseemly dispute; and by 1727 Mrs Pendarves, who had idolized Handel ever since her first meeting with him as a child of ten, was writing to her sister: 'I doubt operas will not survive longer than this winter, they are now at their last gasp; the subscription is expired and nobody will renew it. The directors are always squabbling, and they have so many divisions among themselves that I wonder they have not broken up before.' The novelty had worn off. Something new and different was needed to stimulate the appetite of the idle public in search of amusement and it was found, not at the King's Theatre, but at the old Lincoln's Inn Fields Theatre, run by the son of Christopher Rich.

John Rich had already established himself as the first English Harlequin, adapting the folklore of the Italian *Commedia dell'Arte* to his own skill in miming and introducing the first English pantomime ever to be seen by a London audience. Now, in January 1728, he took a chance on Gay's *The Beggar's Opera* and reaped a fortune. The first performance was received with 'immense applause by a prodigious concourse of the Nobility and Gentry', including the Prime Minister, Sir Robert Walpole; and in March, Pope was writing excitedly to

Swift: 'Mr Gay's opera has acted forty days running and will certainly continue the whole season.' Everyone found it bold and amusing, ribald and colourful with a biting undertone of political and social satire, its realism a refreshing change from the artificiality and elaboration of the Italian opera. The music arranged by Dr Pepusch from old English airs and ballads was tuneful and easy to understand, the highwayman Macheath a glamorous rogue, and the acting of Lavinia Fenton as Polly Peachum delicious. Mr Gay had come into his own, almost in spite of himself.

He was a lazy, self-indulgent, amiable creature; greedy and good-humoured; much loved and spoilt by his friends, who never seemed to mind how much time he spent sponging on them because he was such good company and so amusing. Swift begged him to work harder and continually strove to encourage him; Pope loved him and collaborated with him more than once. But he preferred dozing along in comfort and the convivial evenings he passed with them or with Dr Arbuthnot and the portrait-painter Jervas at a chop-house in Exchange Alley, where he soon admitted to being 'sick with wine' and perfectly happy. He lived for the hour without ever bothering much about the future, though when he failed to obtain an appointment at Court to his liking, he became somewhat peevish and self-pitying, until the success of *The Beggar's Opera* revived his spirits, if not for very long. Satire against the Court and the Government had been obvious enough to the initiated in *The Beggar's Opera*, yet Walpole had sat in a box at the theatre smiling and applauding in a mood of tolerant self-satisfaction. Neither Rich nor Gay expected him to turn suddenly sour over the sequel Gay had been writing while on a visit to Bath, though Macheath had become Morano in the new opera, a more cynical blackguard, more easily recognized as a deliberate portrait of Sir Robert. He acted swiftly

through the Lord Chamberlain: *Polly* was stopped at the
first rehearsal and its production banned at every playhouse.

The shock overwhelmed Gay and made him ill for
months, though some of his friends in opposition to the
Government, defeated of their pleasure in seeing Walpole
traduced on the stage, rushed into battle on his behalf.
The wild and beautiful young Duchess of Queensberry
from her impregnable position at the top of fashionable
society, boldly solicited subscriptions for the publication
of *Polly* in the Queen's own drawing-room and was forbidden the Court, which did not distress her in the least,
for George II, who had succeeded to the throne in 1727,
was loved even less than his father and his Queen was
suspected of having an affair with Walpole. They got the
worst of the quarrel when the Duchess, in answering the
King's letter of dismissal, declared: 'That the Duchess of
Queensberry is surprised and well pleased that the King
hath given her so agreeable a command as to stay away
from Court, where she never came for diversion, but to
bestow a great civility on the King and Queen; she hopes
by such an unprecedented order as this is, that the King
will see as few as he wishes at Court, particularly such as
dare to think or speak the truth.' What the King did when
he received this insulting communication is not recorded,
but the Duchess was quite unabashed, and the Duke of
Queensberry, a mild, inoffensive gentleman, who did
what his Duchess told him to do, also laid down his
appointments at Court, while his wife in a flurry of
indignation, carried Gay off to Hampstead to recuperate.

The scandal that ensued was meat and drink to the
Duchess's highly strung appetite for embarrassing
Walpole's overpowerful ministry. She enjoyed every
moment of it, while Gay continued to protest that he was
innocent of any attempt to harm 'the present happy
establishement of Court and Government'. When he left

Hampstead, he retired into the country with the Duchess and was lucky enough to find a snug nest for the rest of his life in the Duke's various palatial mansions in Oxfordshire, Surrey, Wiltshire and Scotland. The Duke taught him to shoot and took him out riding to improve his health, though he much preferred his idleness and sloth to taking exercise. The Duchess went walking with him and made it her pleasure to cosset him and crown his remaining years with ease.

Her affection for him in a world that cared little for sincerity, was genuine. After his death in 1732, she wrote to her friend the Duchess of Suffolk: 'I often want poor Mr Gay. Nothing evaporates sooner than joy untold, or even told, unless to one so entirely to your interest as he was, who bore an equal share in any satisfaction or dissatisfaction that attended us. I am not in the spleen, though I write thus; on the contrary, it is a sort of pleasure to think over his good qualities. His loss was really great, but it is a satisfaction to have once known such a good man.' And she never forgot him. Half a century later when Walpole and everyone else concerned in the commotion was dead, *Polly* was staged at last and the aged, white-haired Duchess of Queensberry, still wild and beautiful, was carried into the theatre to attend the first performance.

3

WIT
TEMPERED
with
MORALITY

POPE, GAY AND SWIFT, whose friendship remained secure
against all the machinations of their enemies, believed
rightly in some ways that they were living in a cold-
hearted, corrupt age, wherein the individual valued his
selfish pleasure more highly than his personal integrity,
and they sought to cleanse society of its viciousness
through their satirical writings. Addison and Steele, as the
creators of a new form of journalism in the *Tatler* and the
Spectator, had a similar motive, their avowed purpose being
'to enliven morality with wit and to temper wit with
morality'. They scarified the lewd behaviour of the generation preceding their own, ridiculed the fops and the
beaux of the town and extolled the merits of self-control,
politeness and good breeding, seeking to refine the taste

of the public by making virtue attractive. But whereas
Pope and his two friends aimed at high society in the Court
and Government, Addison and Steele addressed themselves to the man in the street, the lawyers, merchants and
businessmen who frequented the coffee houses, and to
those of the country squires who were not, as Lady Mary
Wortley Montagu scornfully suggested, 'wholly insen-
sible to other pleasures than the bottle and the chase,
spending their mornings among the hounds and their
nights with as beastly companions—with what liquor
they can get'.

The friendship between Addison and Steele had begun
during their schooldays at Charterhouse and, according
to Pope in one of his more spiteful moments, was of a
homosexual character. Addison grew up the wiser of the
two, the more authoritative and the more successful in
obtaining preferment at Court and a decent income.
Steele was thriftless, good natured, always in debt and
attractive to women, though when he married Mary
Scurlock, his 'dearest Prue', in 1707, he remained faithful
to her. 'I shall make it the business of my life to make you
easy and happy,' he wrote, and he set her up in a house at
Hampton Wick, which he could not afford to pay for,
with a footman, a gardener, two boys and a woman to wait
on her, while making frantic efforts to settle his confused
financial affairs. These, however, never showed any signs
of improving and kept him so often in town that he was
soon forced to send for Prue to come and stay with friends
in London while he flitted from one lodging to another to
avoid his creditors. He borrowed off everyone he knew
with such cheerfulness that his friends never had the
heart to fail him, and if his wife worried and got peevish,
he usually managed to tease her back into a good temper
by promising her a better and more comfortable life in the
near future. When he took a new house in Bloomsbury
Square in 1712, he wrote: 'You cannot conceive How

pleased I am that I shall have the prettyest house to receive the Prettyest Woman who is the Darling of Richard Steele'; and after ten years of marriage he was still signing his letters 'your Happy Slave and Obedient Husband'.

Meanwhile his collaboration with Addison, if it did not bring him financial stability, gave him the satisfaction of knowing that the reforming influence of the new journalism was achieving the widest possible success. Addison presided and pontificated at Button's Coffee House in Russell Street, Covent Garden, uniting 'merriment with decency and humour with politeness'. His intellectual followers treated him with awe and reverence—all except Pope, who had every reason to suspect him of double-dealing over Tickell's translation of the *Iliad*; and their pleasure in his conversation, which 'reconciled wit and virtue after a long and disastrous separation', kept them awake far into the night, while copies of the *Spectator* were eagerly looked for at the other coffee houses all over London, where men gathered together at their leisure to read the latest news, to gossip and exchange ideas, or to conduct their business in an atmosphere of cordiality and honourable good sense.

'The Coffee Drink prevented Drowsiness' and was advertised as 'an excellent cure for the Spleen, the Dropsy' and several other ills of the body. It was 'a simple, innocent thing to be taken as hot as possibly can be endured, the which will never fetch the Skin off the Mouth or raise any Blisters', and already so popular in England there were more than 500 coffee houses in London alone at this time. Any man on the payment of one penny at the bar, could take a seat by the fire, smoke his pipe in comfort and join in the conversation or not, according to his inclination; and to visitors from abroad the democratic spirit of enjoyment was amazing, Misson remarking on 'the universal liberty of speech among the English' and how you could see 'the blue ribbons and stars of the nobility sitting familiarly with private gentlemen, as if they had left their quality and degrees of distance at home'. All manner of news was exchanged between the customers and they were immune from feminine interference, though the pretty barmaids or *dames de comptoir* in their frilly caps were sometimes an attraction, 'inviting you by their amorous glances into their smoky Territories, to the loss of your sight, or receiving all day long the adoration of the Youth within such and such districts'.

Different coffee houses served different groups of people. There was Lloyd's in Lombard Street, the chief centre in the city for everyone concerned with ships and shipping on the high seas; Garraway's in Exchange Alley, where the first auction sales were held 'by inch of candle'; Jonathen's, also in Exchange Alley, a resort of the stock-jobbers and the scene of wild confusion at the time of the South Sea Bubble crisis; and the Grecian in Devereux Court, a rendezvous for the learned members of the Royal Society, where Ralph Thoresby from Leeds once had the pleasure of watching 'Dr Douglas dissecting a dolphin lately caught in the Thames'.

The poets and men of letters went to Will's and Button's, the artists to Old Slaughter's in St Martin's Lane and Swift to the St James's Coffee House to collect his letters from his beloved 'Stella', while everyone in search of what Steele called 'extraordinary absurdities' went by water to the remote and rural village of Chelsea to visit Don Saltero's. Salter himself, nicknamed Don Saltero by an English Admiral who had sailed the Spanish seas, was something of an exhibitionist. In addition to being a barber, willing to bleed, shave or draw the teeth of his clients free of charge, he played the fiddle, wrote verses and carried a muff close to his face when he went out in the winter. Having once been a valet to Sir Hans Sloane, he had acquired his master's collecting mania and filled his coffee house with relics and curiosities, including such rarities as 'Tiger's tusks, the skeleton of a guinea-pig, the Pope's candle, a fly-cap monkey, Mary Queen of Scots' pincushion and a pair of Nun's stockings'; and although Steele scoffed at this unusual 'museum', it attracted crowds of idle people whose desire for diversion was gratified by the sight of so many varied objects.

Pope, after his quarrel with Addison, gave up going to Button's, preferring the company of Dr Arbuthnot, Gay and his many friends among the nobility. His translation of the *Iliad* had brought him independence from financial anxiety and in 1719 when he settled into his new house at Twickenham with his ageing mother, he was happier and more sure of himself than ever before. The precocious little boy who had once seen Dryden nodding in his chair at Will's, had matured into the sharp-eyed, brilliant poet of *The Rape of the Lock,* that delicious satire on the frivolities of the age shimmering like an exquisite jewel set in the midst of the dull and turgid Augustan verse produced by most of his contemporaries. Dullness Pope could never be accused of; malice, spitefulness and pettiness might cloud his judgment at times, but his was a dual nature, loyal to his friends, gentle, agonizingly sensitive and fiercely courageous. His spirit inhabited 'a tender crazy little carcase' four foot six inches high and permanently deformed by a curvature of the spine. He was racked by physical pain, suffering frightful headaches and recurrent attacks of fever; yet he mastered what he once called 'that long disease, my life', by sheer will-power, and his absorbing search for perfection in his art never wavered.

Unhappily he often looked for a similar perfection in human nature and when he failed to find it reacted violently, love and affection turning to black hatred in his heart and a venomous delight in getting his own back. But as a young man he was full of gaiety and charm in spite of his physical disabilities and his pleasing gallantry recommended him to the Blount sisters, who lived not far away from his father's estate on the edge of Windsor Forest. Teresa was dark with bright eyes and a quick, uncertain temper; Martha, called Patty by her friends, very fair and amiable, with an attractive, sensuous sweetness that appealed strongly to Pope. He wooed them both with undisguised enjoyment, half seriously, half in fun, and finally fell in love with Patty, whose sympathy was constant and unalterable. At the end of his life 'it was very observable that Mrs Blount's coming in gave a new turn of spirits, or a temporary strength to him', so great was her devotion and her power to comfort him.

Quite a different kind of experience, totally lacking in comfort, yet far more vivid and exciting, developed from his other serious love-affair with Lady Mary Wortley Montagu, who had now become a dazzling and witty woman of the world, ambitious for herself and the rather stodgy husband with whom she had eloped in preference to marrying a disagreeable Irish peer with money. Pope met her some time in 1715 before her beauty was ravaged by an attack of smallpox and found her 'a mighty gay and airy person', quick-thinking and delightfully acid in her comments on the Hanoverian Court and society. He was fascinated by her cleverness, her self-assurance and the brilliance of her dark alluring eyes, and for about a year he constantly sought her out when he was in town living with the painter, Jervas. Then to his horror, her husband was appointed Ambassador Extraordinary to the Sublime Porte and she began making preparations to travel to Turkey with him. She was not at all dismayed by the idea of leaving England; she was 'charmed with the thoughts of going into the east' and looked forward to her journey with 'all the pleasure imaginable'. Pope's unconcealed anxiety for her safety was flattering, his anguish at the thought of being separated from her, rather amusing. She begged him to write to her often and promised that she would write to him. Perhaps neither of them realized that distance would lend a dangerous enchantment to the poet's private image of her.

He wrote constantly, following her in his mind's eye across Europe towards the Orient, daring to say on paper all that he had left unsaid in her presence, the fire in his heart and his miserable little body stimulated by his gift of expression and carrying him off into ever wilder and more rhapsodic flights of fancy. He saw her 'happily arrived at the free Region of Adultery' in the mysterious East, practising to sit on the sofa, learning to fold a turban, being bathed and anointed with perfumed oil and lying on a silken bed at Pera. 'Indeed,' he wrote, 'my feelings are so warm, that I fear they can proceed from nothing but what I can't very decently own to you, much less to any other.' Her letters, also, were delightful—diverting, friendly and amusing. Wortley was detained in Vienna, but after a long and perilous journey across the snow-bound plains of Eastern Europe, he and his lady reached Adrianople in April 1717. 'I am now got into a new world, she wrote. 'My garden is full of tall cypress trees, upon the branches of which several couples of true turtles are saying soft things to one another from morning till night. . . .' And before long she had adopted a Turkish costume consisting of a pair of drawers 'of a thin rose-coloured damask brocaded with silver flowers', a wide-sleeved smock 'of fine white silk gauze, through which the shape and the colour of the bosom is very well to be distinguished', a damask waistcoat and a caftan 'of the same stuff with my drawers and exactly fitted to my shape'.

For Pope, sitting at home in the cool of an English spring, this was red-hot fuel to his imagination; for Lady Mary, off again in May to Constantinople, it was simply part of the enjoyment to be found in her strange surroundings. She explored Constantinople very thoroughly, loved her garden and the ravishing view from her windows, had her son inoculated against smallpox by an old Greek woman, disguised herself in a dark cloak to get into St Sophia and was full of curiosity about Turkish manners and morals. She thought Turkish women of the upper classes had 'at least as much wit and civility, nay, liberty, as among us' and was quite of the opinion that the Turks had a right notion of life. 'They consume it in music, gardens and delicate eating, while we are tormenting our brains with some scheme of politics, or studying some science to which we can never attain,' she remarked, adding: 'Considering what short-lived weak animals men are, is there any study so beneficial as the study of present pleasure?' Certainly for her there was none more tantalizing than the hedonism of the East, but she did not then know that her stay in Turkey was almost over; Wortley had not been a success as a diplomat and in 1718 he was abruptly recalled.

Pope's excitement at the thought of her return was quite delirious. 'I long for nothing so much as your Oriental Self,' he wrote. 'I expect to see your soul as much thinner dressed as your body; and that you have left off, as unwieldly and cumbersome, a great many damn'd European habits. Without offence to your modesty be it spoken, I have a burning desire to see your soul stark naked, for I am confident 'tis the prettiest kind of white soul in the universe.' Yet even while he was writing thus of his passionate longing to see her, Pope was, perhaps, a little apprehensive of their reunion. After her return to England he put off meeting her, as if afraid of discovering some flaw in the real Lady Mary that was absent from the romantic image of her which had obsessed him for so long, and when they did come face to face at last, only the excitement of the occasion enabled him to gloss over his

uncertainty and to convince himself that she was as perfect
as he wished her to be.

Lady Mary returned to Court, where again she cut a
brilliant figure and quickly became absorbed in the life of a
fashionable young woman. But Pope persuaded her to
become his close neighbour at Twickenham, and it was
with her in mind that he began laying out his Great Walk
and the subterranean grotto running beneath his villa to
link his Thames-side lawn with his garden on the other
side of the London road. Small though his garden was
compared with Lord Bathurst's at Cirencester and Lord
Burlington's at Chiswick, he was proud, he wrote, 'to
reflect what an honour it is to my Great Walk, that the
finest woman in the world could not stir from it'. None
the less, as time went on, Lady Mary's visits to the
paradise he had so lovingly created for her gradually
became less frequent and before long he was writing to
Gay:

Ah friend, 'tis true—this truth you lovers know—
In vain my structures rise, my gardens grow,
In vain fair Thames reflects the double scenes
Of hanging mountains, and of sloping greens:
Joy lives not here; to happier seats it flies,
And only dwells where WORTLEY casts her eyes.

Then suddenly in 1723, disaster struck the poet down.
Did he make love to her at some ill-chosen moment and
did she, 'in spite of her utmost endeavour to be angry and
look grave, burst into an immoderate fit of laughter'? Or
did they quarrel over some sheets she borrowed from his
mother and returned unwashed? Whatever the cause it
was the end of Pope's joy in her company. Lady Mary
brushed him off like a tiresome fly and continued to give
amusing parties at her villa for Senesino, Bononcini, Lord
Burlington and the Duke of Wharton. Pope withdrew

into his grotto to brood over his stricken heart and five years later, with a ferocity and a violence that showed the unutterable depth of his hurt feelings, attacked her in one of the most obscene set of verses he ever wrote. Lady Mary deserved it; experience should have warned her that her poetic adorer was not really a fly at all, but a wasp with a nasty sting.

Pope's passionate pleasure in his garden—quite apart from his original purpose of enticing Lady Mary to linger there—was a manifestation of the *avant-garde* taste of his generation; for if his friend and neighbour at Chiswick, the Earl of Burlington, was the chief protagonist of the new elegance in architecture and garden design, it was Pope who was responsible for spreading the gospel of Palladianism. He believed that the only way for the high-born aristocrat to achieve a distinctive moral superiority over his fellow-men was to cultivate an ultra-refined taste in the arts; it was his duty to eschew all vulgarity and needless ornament, 'to consult the genius of the place in all', to blend art with nature and find the correct balance between the two as in the perfect form of a poem.

Lord Burlington did precisely this. Lord Bathurst, Pope's other great friend in Gloucestershire, did not always quite live up to the desired degree of moral superiority, but he did set out to create an ideal garden at Cirencester Park by uprooting the formal parterres of his ancestors and bringing the woods round his estate into the general scheme of arrangement, so that park and gardens were linked together by one superb avenue of trees six miles long. Pope's advice and his own instinct guided him towards the beautiful effects he achieved with his 'silvan bowers, secret glades and elysian groves', for Bathurst was not an intellectual scholar versed in the classics; he was extremely gay and lovable, immoderately fond of dancing and of wine and snuff, generous to his friends, absolutely to be trusted and a great lover with an uninhibited delight in his own capacity for 'getting children at home and abroad'. Even at the age of eighty-five he had, according to Laurence Sterne, 'all the wit and promptness of a man of thirty . . . a disposition to be pleased and a power to please others beyond whatever I know'; and at ninety-one, after his eldest son, the pious and abstemious Lord Chancellor, had withdrawn from the dining-room, he is said to have exclaimed: 'Come, now the old gentleman's gone, let us crack another bottle!'

Lord Bathurst's robust constitution was unimpaired by his ardent love of pleasure. Lord Burlington, a younger man by ten years, was more delicate and of quite a different character: less ebullient, even somewhat frigid, but with his taste, his talents and his learning much closer to Pope's ideal of aristocratic superiority. He made his first tour of Italy at the age of twenty, with an equipage of fine carriages and horses, several little dogs, a tutor and a large retinue of servants. Architecture was not then his predominant interest. He had a passion for music, hiring harpsichords wherever he went—two in Rome, one in Florence and another in Pisa—besides persuading Pietro Castrucci, an Italian violinist, to join his suite of attendants. He bought paintings by Domenichino, Carlo Maratta and Pascoline, a porphyry vase and some antique busts, and on his way home through Paris, two harpsichords, a bass viol, a set of silver dessert-baskets, fourteen pairs of gloves and 'a comb for the little dogs'. Back in London he entertained Handel and guaranteed £1000 towards the foundation of the Royal Academy of Music, began to make alterations to Burlington House and went down to Chiswick to look round the gardens of the Jacobean mansion he had inherited there. But it was not until 1715 that he came upon two large volumes which stirred his interest in architectural design. One was Colen Campbell's

Vitruvius Britannicus calling for a return to 'the antique simplicity' of Inigo Jones, and the other a translation of Giacomo Leoni's *The Architecture of A Palladio*. The inspiration of these two folios was immediate. Burlington dismissed Wren's follower James Gibbs and put the alterations to Burlington House into the hands of Colen Campbell, and in 1719, again set off for Italy to study the Palladian villas of the Veneto, taking with him, 'to draw all ye fine buildings', a young artist from Yorkshire named William Kent.

It was the beginning of a quite extraordinary friendship between the patrician Earl and the almost illiterate son of a coach-painter, of a collaboration which changed the whole attitude of the aristocracy towards a more restrained taste in the display of their wealth. 'I hope, by his Lordship's encorgement and other Gentlemen, who may have a better gusto than that damned gusto that's been for this sixty years past,' Kent wrote—and although his grammar never improved, his hope was entirely justified by events. The neo-Baroque style of Wren, Vanbrugh and Hawksmoor suffered an eclipse; it was considered old-fashioned, extravagant and absurd. The vulgar display of the *nouveau-riche* Duke of Chandos at Cannons with the statues, fountains and arcades in his gardens, the aviaries filled with Muscovy ducks, flamingoes and other exotic birds and the hot-houses laden with pineapples, pawpaws, guavas and tamarinds, merely exhibited the ill-breeding, the pride and the false grandeur of this upstart creature. Only the newly discovered Palladian style of classical correctness and proportion was suitable to the proper aristocratic sensibility and moral superiority of the new age. For in art as in life, harmony, symmetry and a dignified elegance were the virtues to be sought and man, by creating beautiful houses and beautiful gardens, could achieve a synthesis of the discordant elements in himself.

Thus Lord Burlington with his Olympian calm became the absolute exemplar of the new trend in aesthetic
and moral feeling expressed by the Palladian theory,
though Kent, whose business it was to translate the theory
into practice through his actual designs, was the exact
opposite. The Earl gave him his own apartments in
Burlington House, fondly called him 'Kentino' or 'The
Signor' and apparently was not in the least put out by
his boisterous behaviour. Indeed his own austere and
ascetic temperament seemed to revel in the easy-going,
indolent charm of his pleasure-loving protégé, who 'often
gave orders when he was full of claret' and at Chiswick
in the absence of his patron, frequently 'lolled and drank
beneath the trees, solacing himself with syllabubs, dam-
sels and other benefits of nature'. Even Burlington's
marriage in 1721 to Lady Dorothy Saville, a daughter of
the Earl of Halifax, made no difference to Kent's freedom
of the household. Herself an exceptionally good draughts-
woman with a flair for caricaturing, she accepted him and
loved him and, in spite of her own fiery temper, deferred
to his ideas in decoration, furniture design and painting.
'Kentino' could do no wrong and his talents were so
extremely versatile that there was no one to equal him,
though when Lady Burlington endeavoured to further
his reputation at Court she did not have much success. 'I
took ye liberty to differ with Mr Bridgman,' she wrote,
referring to the Queen's gardener and his works at
Richmond. 'He said that 3 slopes made it look bigger; I
think one would be not only handsomer, but look (in his
style) more grande.' Mr Bridgeman was not impressed by
her criticism and neither was the Queen, who had her own
very definite ideas about gardening and was only prevented
from annexing the whole of St James's Park as a private
garden to the Palace when she asked Sir Robert Walpole
how much it would cost her and he dryly answered: 'Only
three crowns, your Majesty.'

Kent, meanwhile, was given a free hand in the Burlingtons' garden at Chiswick; and in 1725 when a fire destroyed part of the old Jacobean mansion, the Earl decided to build a new villa, standing a little apart but linked to the old house. Here was the opportunity for this gifted amateur to express the knowledge he had acquired through his own pleasure in studying the classical forms of Palladio—and he took it brilliantly. His design was by no means a slavish copy of the Villa Rotonda at Vicenza; it was an exquisite creation of his own, skilfully adapted to its purpose as a setting for the works of art he had collected and to the landscape of Kent's garden surrounded by the green fields of Middlesex. Pope said it was 'the finest thing this glorious sun has shin'd upon' and Burlington himself loved it so much that, when the business of his other estates in Yorkshire and in London took him away from it, he could not get home quick enough. 'He had every quality of a genius and artist, except envy,' Horace Walpole declared. 'Never was protection and great wealth more generously and more judiciously diffused than by this great person.'

Both as a patron and as an architect, Burlington surpassed all his contemporaries, except Lord Herbert, another highly gifted aristocratic gentleman of leisure, who designed Marble Hill House at Twickenham for Mrs Henrietta Howard, the mistress of George II when he was still Prince of Wales. Mrs Howard's life had not been easy. 'Good sense, good breeding and good nature were qualities which even her enemies could not deny her,' but her husband, a son of the Earl of Suffolk, was a vicious, drunken brute, so improvident with money that she once had to cut her glorious chestnut hair off and sell it to pay for a dinner party he gave in Hanover. Her association with the Prince of Wales was not much happier, since he did not love her, he only cherished 'the silly idea' that a prince without a mistress cut a poor figure in the eyes of his courtiers, and although his wife, the Princess Caroline, was reputed to have said that she preferred her 'good Howard' to any other rival in her husband's affections, she was often less than kind to her, finding countless opportunities to humiliate her and to make her attendance at Court a misery.

So it was with joy and relief that poor Henrietta Howard set about planning her escape to Twickenham after the Prince had grudgingly settled a little money on her. Only her closest friends—Pope and Gay and Lord Herbert—were allowed into the secret. Pope busied himself with drawing plans for the layout of her garden by the riverside, while Lord Herbert, with the help of Roger Morris, started building her villa in the Palladian style. It was simple, elegant and spacious without being overlarge, and thus eminently suited to her circumstances. Even so, she was seldom able to enjoy it until seven years later, when fortune at last turned a more favourable eye on her with the death of her father-in-law, who left some of his property in trust for her, and her elevation to the peerage. By then the Prince of Wales had become King and it was impossible for his consort to treat the Countess of Suffolk as if she were still plain Mrs Howard; etiquette demanded her promotion from a Woman of the Bedchamber to Mistress of the Robes with a decent remuneration.

'Everything as yet promises more happiness for the latter part of my life than I have yet had the prospect of,' she wrote joyfully to Gay. 'I shall now often visit Marble Hill . . . and I shall see it without the dread of being obliged to sell it in answer to the engagements I had put myself under to avoid a greater evil.' This, too, the last impediment to her happiness, was removed within a year or two by the death of her dissipated husband, and shortly afterwards the Countess of Suffolk was able to retire from the Court altogether to live in comfort and in quiet at Marble Hill, marrying an old admirer of hers, the Hon George Berkeley, who devoted himself to her welfare, and enjoying the pleasure of Horace Walpole's company after he had settled at Strawberry Hill.

Lord Herbert, who succeeded his father, the 8th Earl of Pembroke, in 1733 and became the master of Wilton House, the superb Inigo Jones mansion in Wiltshire filled with marble busts, paintings, rare books, gems and intaglios collected by his cultured ancestors, continued to visit the Countess of Suffolk at Twickenham, though at one time the long friendship between them was somewhat strained. For Pembroke was a curious mixture—pugnacious, public-spirited, honest and kind, but deplorably hot-tempered and by no means the restrained type of aristocrat Pope admired. He could rant and rage and blaspheme until his victims trembled with terror and then forget all about it with a laughing, lovable generosity, though often he was plunged into gloom and remorse by his own ungovernable fierceness. He was keen on hunting and shooting and country matters and combined this love of sport with an intellectual curiosity, which made him an energetic member of the Royal Society and a connoisseur of the arts. He supported the Academy of Painting in St Martin's Lane, commissioned busts from Scheemakers and Roubiliac and was so eccentric that he once took to vegetarianism and was seen in the streets of Paris wearing a bag-wig filled with watercress and beetroot, which he extracted from time to time to nibble when he was hungry. He loved his horses and his dogs, and his wife, whom he nicknamed Rib from the story of Adam and Eve; and, in addition to Marble Hill, he designed a house in Richmond Park for the King and the exquisite Palladian bridge at Wilton. Nothing so sensitive or so pure in outline had ever been conceived before; nothing of the Earl of Pembroke's rage or his eccentricity was visible in its perfect form. His bridge was a masterpiece, surpassing the art of

Palladio himself, and a glorious symbol of his own individual taste and imagination.

It was copied at Stowe, at Hagley, at Amesbury and at
Prior Park, the superb Palladian house built by Ralph
Allen overlooking the city of Bath, which by then had
become the most fashionable of all the spas and water-
ing-places in England. Ralph Allen himself, in addition
to reforming the postal service, played a considerable part
in the development of Bath. Though a self-made man, he
was generous and civic-minded and took pleasure in
spending his money for the benefit of the city. He owned
and worked the local quarries of soft, honey-coloured
stone and encouraged John Wood and his son to transform the dirty, narrow streets of the old town by the Avon
into elegant thoroughfares, squares and crescents of
houses as harmonious as those designed by Palladio to
adorn the banks of the Brenta and the Po.

Accommodation for the modish visitors in search of a
cure for their ailments was urgently needed. The hot
springs of ancient British and Roman origin were widely
advertised as 'a Sovereign Remedy against all Faintings,
Sweatings, Lowness of Spirits etc . . . or Disorders pro-
ceeding from Intemperance, eating of Fruit, drinking of
bad wine or any other poysonous or crude liquors'; and as
intemperance was a habit among the rich, there were
naturally a great number of sufferers who hoped to benefit
from drinking the waters or bathing in them. There were
also hordes of doctors, quacks and charlatans, like a
swarm of horrid bees buzzing round the poor invalids,
with their nostrums, their cupping and bleeding and other
nauseous prescriptions. But if there was not much fun
to be had from them or from floating under a canvas
garment shaped like a bell-tent in the scalding and rather
grubby waters of the King's Bath, there were other diversions designed to relieve the tedium of undergoing a cure,
for which one very remarkable man was responsible.

Beau Nash was a professional gamester. He arrived in Bath in 1702 with one guinea in the pocket of his tired brocaded coat and nothing to recommend him except his swaggering optimism. Very soon, however, he had ingratiated himself with a number of important people and had become Master of Ceremonies with absolute authority over the entertainments he devised to please the crowds arriving every summer. His rules in the Pump Room, the Assembly Rooms and the Gaming Rooms were strict. There was to be 'no crowding of the Gentlemen before the Ladies at the Ball, no appearing in a Morning before the Ladies in Gowns and Caps, no whispering of Lies and Scandals, no Ill-manners between the Young and the Old.' Gentlemen were forbidden to wear boots or swords in the ball room and ladies charged to leave their aprons at home; and the Beau took care to see that his Code of Behaviour was observed. When the Duchess of Queensberry once appeared in a point-lace apron which had cost her 500 guineas, the Beau snatched it off her and threw it to one of the waiting-women standing by the wall, and it was not he who apologized to the Duchess, but the fiery Duchess who apologized to him.

The vigilance of this extraordinary man with a brandy-coloured face crowned by a brown wig and a large, three-cornered white hat, was concentrated in his prominent, rather watery blue eyes. Persons of high rank and fashion quailed beneath his quizzical stare, and rude country squires and their wives, assuming an air of modish gentility, behaved with unusual decorum. The Beau insisted on politeness from everyone, even on the con-descension of ladies of quality towards the well-to-do tradesmen and their wives and daughters, who subscribed to the balls and concerts. He made arrangements for ladies to be carried home in their sedan-chairs 'to prevent Disturbances and Inconveniencies to Themselves and Others'. He had the streets paved and lit by lanthorns 'as

it shall grow dark until 12 o'clock at night', to discourage
footpads and other lawless persons. And the Gaming
Rooms at Bath were never the scenes of the drunken,
hectic brawling that went on everywhere else; they were
conducted with decency and discipline. Here again, the
wearing of swords was forbidden and in consequence
gentlemen quarrelling over the dice were less likely to
settle their disputes in a duel on the spot or on Coombe
Down the next morning; the Beau gave them time to cool
off and a serious lecture as well, and few of them dared to
incur his displeasure.

He was King of Bath and he knew it. Not even Princess
Amelia, the daughter of George II, could succeed in
persuading him to extend the ball she was enjoying so
much beyond the hour of eleven. When she warned him
by saying: 'Remember, *I* am a Princess,' he answered:
'Yes, madam, but *I* reign here and *my* laws must be kept.'
So the one more country-dance the Princess longed for
under the dazzling chandeliers in the Assembly Room was
denied her, and the Beau's prestige and authority continued to increase until he got involved in a lawsuit under
the new Gaming Act, which ruined his reputation and
robbed him of his personal fortune, but did not greatly
trouble the *beau-monde* still seeking pleasure in the
glorious city of honey-coloured elegance that he had done
so much to make famous.

Everyone who was anyone went there—Pope and the
Blount sisters, Gay and Dr Arbuthnot, Addison, Steele,
the Duchess of Marlborough, Lord Chesterfield, the Earl
of Chatham and the Methodist Countess of Huntingdon;
and those who were nobody hoped by being seen there,
they might be taken for somebody. They could stroll on
the North Parade on summer afternoons among the high-
class visitors or eat buns for breakfast in the Spring
Gardens; they could gossip for hours and drink tea in the
Pump Room, or listen to the orchestra playing under Dr

E

Herschel, the future Astronomer Royal, provided he did not suddenly drop his violin and rush away to view the stars through his home-made telescope. They had endless leisure and nothing whatever to do, except to enjoy themselves.

4

MOB
AMUSEMENTS

THE SPAS AND wells were popular centres of pleasure all through the eighteenth century. Besides Bath and Tunbridge Wells and Epsom, several medicinal springs had been discovered in the hills surrounding London and exploited with considerable success. At Hampstead the chalybeate waters on the Wells Estate were recommended by Dr Gibbons, a physician who lived in the neighbourhood. At first they were bottled in the near-by Flask Tavern and sent to an apothecary at the Eagle and Child in Fleet Street to be sold at 3d a flask. Then John Duffield built an Assembly Room to hold 500 people and started advertising in the *Postman*: 'A Consort of bothe vocal and instrumental Musick, with some particular performance of bothe kinds by the best Masters to begin at 10 o'clock precisely', stating categorically that the moon would be shining that night and therefore the nobility and gentry need have no fear of the footpads lurking in fields on the way north from Marylebone. Tickets for the concerts were 1s each and for a time Mr Duffield's entertainments in the sweet air of Hampstead were a popular attraction to the *beau-monde*, while higher up the hill at the Upper Flask Tavern, the Kit-Cat Club held its summer meetings.

But Hampstead had its ups and downs as a fashionable resort and its prestige declined sharply when the riff-raff of the city, the gamblers and loose women of the town found their way there and began to outnumber the upper-class visitors. A raffling shop was set up by a doubtful legal gentleman under the name of his maid or his mistress, Mrs Sisley, and the Great Room was converted into a chapel where irregular marriages were conducted for a fee of 5s or the price of a dinner in the gardens; and although the new Assembly Room and Ball Room built in 1727 attracted a better class of company again, Fanny Burney's Evelina some years later found the Long Room 'without ornament, elegance or any other sort of singularity' and the young men who 'begged the favour of hopping a dance with her', highly impertinent.

At Pancridge, or St Pancras Wells, not far away, undesirable characters were excluded from the Pump Room and the House of Entertainment, but 'neat wines, curious Punch, Dorchester and Ringwood beers' were available to those who preferred a stronger stimulant than the waters, and cows were kept 'to accommodate ladies and gentlemen with new milk and cream and syllabubs in the greatest perfection'. The springs were advertised as 'a powerful antidote against the rising of the vapours and a sovereign help to Nature', and the gardens here were very extensive with bowling-alleys, fish ponds and long straight walks shaded by avenues of trees, one of them set aside for ladies wishing to enjoy a certain privacy from the importunities of the opposite sex.

Elsewhere the sexes mingled happily enough and with absolute freedom. They filled the Musick-house built by Mr Sadler after he had discovered 'the excellent steel waters' of an old well when he was digging for gravel in Islington in 1683; and they flocked to the rival establish-

ment on the opposite side of the New River Head known
as Islington Spa or the New Tunbridge Wells. Mr Sadler
and his successor, Mr Rosoman, charged a guinea for the
whole season and provided cheesecakes and ale as well as
the bitter waters of Aesculapius for the visitors arriving
at any time after ten o'clock in the morning. Their
entertainments at the Musick-house included concerts of
kettle-drums and hautboys, acrobatic turns with clowns
and tumblers, rope-dancers, pantomime and aquatic
spectacles. But Mr Langley at the New Tunbridge Wells
opposite, not to be outdone, put a rhinoceros on exhibition, and round about 1733 the New Tunbridge Wells
reached the height of its glory, its pleasures described in a
song called *The Charms of Dishabille*:

> Behold the walks, a chequer'd shade
> In the gay pride of green array'd:
> How bright the sun, the air how still!
> In wild confusion there we view
> Red ribbons grouped with aprons blue;
> Scrapes, curtsies, nods, winks, smiles and frowns,
> Lords, milkmaids, duchesses and clowns,
> In their all various *dishabille*.

Princess Amelia and her sister Princess Caroline, Lády
Sunderland and Pope's Wortley Montagu were among the
ladies to be seen enjoying their leisure in the gardens after
breakfast and one young girl writing to a friend, described
the spa as 'a very Romantick place', though she found the
waters made her 'vastly cold and hungary'. Rank and
fashion rubbed shoulders with the dandified sparks from
the Inns of Court, the pretty seamstresses and the well-to-
do shopkeepers of the city; but before long, as at Hampstead, the gamesters, pickpockets and panders began to
invade the green walks and the card room, and the spa
fell into disrepute.

There was no stopping the mob and their greed for mischief. They emerged like ants from the underworld of London and swarmed into the better-class districts to mingle with fashionable society and tempt the weaker sort into debauchery. They profaned the streets with their loud cries and disorderly behaviour, mixing with the aristocrats on their way to Court and the ladies of quality strolling in the Mall; and they were ever on the look-out for a purse or a gold watch they could pinch, or for the chance of insinuating themselves into the good graces of anyone foolish enough to stop and listen. Servants blackmailed their mistresses and stole from their masters; footmen, chairmen, shop assistants and tavern-keepers were all in league with each other to mulct the rich and feed on their insobriety, and no one was safe at night from being set upon by footpads or highwaymen. Horace Walpole returning by moonlight from Lord Holland's country house to his home in Arlington Street, was stopped in Hyde Park by two of the most notorious of 'Diana's Foresters', Plunket and Maclean, and the latter's pistol went off by accident, sending the bullet so nearly through Walpole's head that it stunned him and went through the roof of the coach. Afterwards he made a joke of it and said the whole affair was conducted 'with the greatest good-breeding on both sides', but Walpole was a past-master at turning the incidents of everyday life into a good story to amuse his friends.

As a resident in Arlington Street, he suffered every year from 'the unceasing uproar' caused by the mob that assembled for two weeks in the summer on the other side of Piccadilly at May Fair. Originally established by James II for the serious purposes of trading, the fair had long since declined into a rowdy, disreputable place of entertainment similar to the other great fairs at Smithfield and in Southwark, which had both become by this time an excuse for presenting 'Loose, Idle and Disorderly People with Plays, Interludes and Puppet Shows' instead of a market for the sale of merchandise. May Fair died out in 1764 when the ground was developed into a fashionable residential area. Bartholomew, the oldest, the biggest and the most popular of all the fairs, continued into the nineteenth century; it lasted for two weeks in August, drawing immense crowds of all classes, even royalty, for in 1740 Frederick Prince of Wales, 'dressed in a ruby-coloured frock coat very richly guarded with gold lace', toured the fair by torchlight, accompanied by a numerous suite of gentlemen.

Booths were set up all round Smithfield for the theatrical diversions put on by William Penkethman, the leading comedian at Drury Lane and by Thomas Doggett, the actor whose name is still associated with the coat and badge rowed for annually by the Thames watermen. Penkethman got hold of a large elephant, sitting in state on its back to advertise his performances; and at Doggett's Booth, 'over against the Hosier Lane end of Bartholomew Fair', a very elaborate new droll was set out on the playbill as: 'THE DISTRESS'D VIRGIN or *the Unnatural Parents*. Being a True History of the *Fair Maid of the West*, or THE LOVING SISTERS. With the Comical Travels of *Poor Trusty* in Search of his *Master's Daughter*, and his Encounter with *Three Witches*'—a feast of entertainment, which also included a 'A Variety of Comick Dances and Songs with Scenes and Machines, the like never seen in the Fair before', specially designed to appeal to a sophisticated audience, 'a commodious passage for the Quality and Coaches' being announced, 'with Lights and People to conduct them to their places'.

The actors did very well out of their booths at the fair and in competition with each other provided ever more 'stately and surprising Scenes: as a Rowling Sea, bearing a large Ship under Sayl, with *Neptune*, Mermaids, Dolphins, etc., and a Prospect of a Moorish Country, [apparently] so swarming with Rats and Mice, that they over run the King and Queen's Table at Dinner'. But these were the more exotic and expensive spectacles. For the gaping and illiterate mob there were the puppet-shows, Merry Andrews, rope-dancers, tumblers, necro-mancers, dancing bears, dogs and monkeys, the ginger-bread and toy stalls and the freaks. At the Hart's Horn's Inn in Pye Corner was to be seen 'a little Farey Woman, lately come from Italy, being Two Foot Two Inches high, the shortest that was ever seen in England and no ways Deform'd', and next door to the Golden Hart in West Smithfield 'an Admirable Work of Nature, a Woman having three Breasts and each of them affording Milk at one time or differently according as they are made use of'.

Nothing of the refinement or the elegance of the new age ever penetrated the saturnalian spirit of the fairs. The noise of the drums and the flutes, the penny-whistles and the trumpets deafened the ear of the seething rabble intent on amusing itself and the stench of roast sucking-pig hung on the foetid air like a burnt cloud. Southwark was equally uproarious, covering a large area extending from St Margaret's Court at the south end of London Bridge to St George's Church and the old Mint and lasting for fourteen days in September. A procession of the Lord Mayor and his sheriffs clad in their scarlet and fur-trimmed gowns, rode round the fair to declare it open, before returning to Bridge House where a great banquet of turtle soup, roast beef, fat geese and stuffed capons was provided for them. But as at Smithfield, the trading aspect of the fair was forgotten when the actors set up their booths in Blue Maid Alley or at the Queen's Arms Yard, backing on to the Marshalsea debtors' prison; and in 1743, when the inhabitants of Southwark complained of the lewd and disorderly persons assembled and of the consequent 'great noises and disturbances', a law was passed limiting the entertainment at the fair, though far

Scene from 'The Beggar's Opera' by William Hogarth, 1728

Cockfighting by William Hogarth, *c.* 1750

Covent Garden in 1737 by B. Nebot

Islington Spa or New Tunbridge Wells in 1733

A View of Bath in 1773 by John Robert Cozens

The Rotunda at Ranelagh by Canaletto, 1754

The Gardens at Stourhead in 1777 by C. W. Bampfyld

Mr and Mrs Robert Andrews by Thomas Gainsborough, *c.* 1750

from succeeding in its purpose, it caused a riot, ending in the defeat of the city constables and a great number of broken heads and bloody noses.

All attempts to bring order and decency into the lives of the people inhabiting the ramshackle, neglected quarters of the city were, in fact, doomed to failure, at least until 1748 when the novelist, Henry Fielding, a man of humanitarian views far in advance of his time, became a magistrate and organized the parish constables, later known as the Bow Street Runners, into a forceful arm of the law, besides conducting his court with integrity and an absence of corruption hitherto unknown. His was the first honest effort to make some progress towards relieving the distress rampant in the crime-infested neighbourhood which came under his jurisdiction; he had imagination and was a very shrewd judge of character, but he knew what he was up against. He described the mob as 'that very large and powerful body which forms the fourth estate of this community' and he knew they took a cruel delight in punishing each other, in whipping and ducking the thieves and prostitutes among them or in pelting the prisoners set in the pillory with bricks and stones, dead cats, rotten eggs and filth grabbed up from the gutter.

Vice and corruption, brutality and beastliness were the only kinds of enjoyment the rabble really understood and drink was their only comfort. De Saussure, an aristocratic French visitor to England, was shocked by the amount of liquor consumed by every class of person he came across, and Benjamin Franklin, working as a printer in London in the 1720s, noted: 'My companion at press drank every day a pint of beer before breakfast, a pint at breakfast, a pint between breakfast and dinner, a pint in the afternoon about 6 o'clock and another pint when he had done his day's work.' And besides this, workmen went to the taverns on Saturday night to collect their wages, and unless their wives came as well to guard them against temptation, frequently gambled and drank their money away before returning home empty-handed.

Yet beer drinking, however excessive, was harmless compared with the lust for gin drinking that developed from this time onwards, the distilling industry, according to Defoe, being 'one of the most essential things to support the landed interest . . . and therefore to be preserved and tenderly used'. Fielding, after two years' experience at Bow Street Police Court, saw things rather differently. 'Gin is the principal Sustenance (if it may be so called) of more than a hundred thousand persons in this Metropolis,' he wrote. 'Many of these Wretches there are, who swallow Pints of this Poison within the Twenty Four Hours; the dreadful Effects of which I have the Misfortune every day to see, and to smell too.' There was not very much he could do about it. One house in every four was a gin shop, open all day and all night, and the intoxication induced by Madame Geneva, Strip-me-naked or Blue Ruin as it was variously called, if it created a temporary feeling of rapture, led inevitably to the degradation pictured by Hogarth in his celebrated painting, 'Gin Lane'.

No one knew more of life as it was lived in the stinking back-alleys of Seven Dials and Covent Garden than Hogarth; no one was more aware of the teeming populace in the streets, of the chaotic mixture of rough gaiety, good nature and sordid distress. He saw the pretty little milliners tripping along with their bandboxes and their alluring glances, the red-faced applewomen and the Billingsgate wenches, wet to the elbows in slimy fish; the blind ballad-singers, the barber with his wig-boxes and a comb stuck in his hair, the boy chimneysweeps, the child prostitutes and the skinny guttersnipes weaving in and out among the gilt coaches of the gentry, the sedans and the offal carts. Himself a cockney, but of middle-class origin, London was his heaven and his hell. It had colour, humour, cheerfulness and wit, and it was putrid, crapulous, squalid and reeking with immorality.

Hogarth was born in Bartholomew Close, the son of an impoverished schoolmaster, and grew up into a sturdy, snub-nosed, plain little man of a somewhat pugnacious disposition, ever at odds with his own genius and the lack of recognition it received from the cultured aristocracy. He ran away with the gentle daughter of Sir James Thornhill, the successful painter responsible for decorating the dome of St Paul's and the ceiling of Greenwich Hospital, and was happy enough in the quiet domestic life they enjoyed in Leicester Fields with his dogs and his chosen circle of friends. He was fond of Fielding and his blind half-brother Sir John, who also became a magistrate; of the genial and philanthropic Captain Coram, who built the Foundling Hospital; of Cox, the auctioneer in Covent Garden, and of Jonathen Tyers, the proprietor of Vauxhall Gardens; and he was on good terms with many of his fellow artists, Samuel Scott, Francis Hayman and Joseph Highmore. But he was none the less constantly provoked and humiliated by the upper-class *cognoscenti,* whose taste ruled the world of art. He hated the refined elegance of the Palladian style, was jealous of Kent's success and bitterly opposed to the prevailing fashion for collecting 'old black paintings' as he furiously called the works of the Italian masters. He thought he could do as well as any Domenichino or Carlo Maratta, though his own history paintings in the antique style were a failure and he was hurt and dismayed by the derision they excited, hitting out wildly at his critics and making himself look rather foolish in the process. His portraits did not gain him any great favour either, except with his middle-class sitters, for he refused to flatter anyone or to become one of 'the phizz-mongers' he despised. And his closely observed scenes of the life he saw all around him, motivated by a strong moral fervour, were only accepted for all the wrong reasons—for the sensational delinquencies they revealed and the actual portraits in them of the well-known bad characters of the underworld, rather than as the warning against licentiousness that he intended.

The *Harlot's Progress* and the *Rake's Progress* were an indictment of the idle, greedy, pleasure-loving dissipations of the educated men and women who should have known better, no less than of the gin-sodden populace that battened on them. His stupid Tom Rakewell, posing as a patron of the arts, was fleeced and put upon by the bad company he got into, driven by his senseless gambling and debauchery to the Fleet Prison and finally to a fearful death among the lunatics at Bedlam. Mother Needham in her smart-looking hood and cape, fondling the fresh young Mary Hackabout upon her arrival in London from the country in the first plate of the *Harlot's Progress,* was a recognizable portrait of one of the many venal procuresses inhabiting the once fashionable but now degenerate area of Covent Garden. Moll King was another, whose notorious house was a feature of the Piazza, where 'every species of human kind that intemperance, idleness, necessity or curiosity could assemble together . . . were to be found nightly indulging their festivities.' Noblemen went there after leaving Court, 'in full dress with swords and bags and rich brocaded silk coats', to gratify their not very noble instincts of the flesh and the devil, and a certain Mr Apreece, 'a tall thin man in rich dress' was Moll King's constant customer, creeping in, as he thought, unobserved through a side-door.

The front windows of the bagnios under the Piazza were filled from seven at night until five o'clock in the morning with impudent trollops in fine silks and satins or in very little clothing at all, lying in wait for the gentlemen returning from the play at Drury Lane or the new Theatre Royal in Bow Street built by John Rich. A guide called *The Man of Pleasure's Kalendar for the Year,* giving a list of the more expensive courtesans and a detailed account of their charms and their qualifications besides telling where they could be found, was published annually by a Mr Harris and sold in great numbers. Flagellation, sodomy and every kind of aberration could be gratified for money; but the worst characters of the town, according to one writer, made the Rose Tavern in Russell Street 'the headquarters of midnight orgies and drunken broils, where murderous assaults frequently occurred and were settled in the dark, underground cellars'.

The young Mohocks and the lecherous old libertines like 'Colonel' Francis Charteris, who 'in spite of age and infirmities persisted in the practice of every human vice', scoured the district in pursuit of their prey. Sir Francis Dashwood and the rakes of the Hell Fire Club, when not indulging in their blasphemous revels at Medmenham Abbey near Marlow, roved from one brothel to another, causing havoc among the women for sale. And on one occasion three fairly respectable friends of Horace Walpole's got into trouble. 'Constables broke into a bagnio at Covent Garden and took up Jack Spencer, Mr Stewart and Lord George Graham, and would have thrust them into the Round House with the poor women, if they had not been worth more than eighteenpence,' he reported complacently; but no doubt the constables themselves were wary, for very often when they refused to be bribed into a quiescent humour, they were beaten up by the delinquent gentlemen they attempted to apprehend and the consequent free-for-all could develop into a bloody battle with bits and pieces of torn clothing and broken weapons left lying in the litter of the morning, when the country people from the villages of Islington and Brompton invaded the market with their mounds of vegetables and their nosegays of flowers.

A love of fighting was inherent in the English and part of the freedom they boasted of. As with their passion for gambling, it ran like a train of gunpowder through the whole nation, inflaming the behaviour of the highest lords and the lowest dregs of society and bringing them together in a way that bewildered and astonished foreign visitors to London. Gambling was not so much a vice among the rich as a habit, like snuff-taking. Cards and dice and speculation in stocks and trading ventures were only one manifestation of the sport to be had in winning— or losing—large sums of money. They gambled on anything and everything—horse-racing, cock-fighting, boxing, wrestling, even cricket in its early days; they gambled on their capacity to drink each other under the table, on the result of an election to Parliament, on the sex of their unborn children or on the chances of a wife leaving her husband. And for the poor, gambling was almost a necessity, the only outlet for their aggressive energy. The old sailors at Greenwich Hospital, when they had nothing to do with their tedious hours of leisure, set their lice to run races on the table with mugs of beer as the stakes. A man ran naked round St James's Park for a wager of thirty guineas, and at Moorfields two women wrestled with each other in ten dishevelled bouts of fury while the spectators yelled their bets out loud. Boys were put into the ring to fight with their naked fists and Misson, while in London, was amazed when he saw 'the Duke of Grafton at Fisticuffs in the open Street with a coachman, whom he lamb'd most horribly'.

All arguments were settled in this brutal way, if not with fists, with swords and staves; and there were hideous, bloodthirsty confrontations staged in the Bear Garden at Hockley-in-the-Hole, called Trials of Skill, in which one professional gladiator hacked at another with a broadsword while the spectators, 'thrusting, justling, elbowing and sweating', shrieked with joy and pelted the loser with rotten vegetables. Even women fought each other with two-handed swords as an amusement for the

public. One of these Amazons, sitting next to von
Uffenbach, a German visitor to the Bear Garden, told him
she had once fought another woman 'without stays and
in nothing but a shift' and gave him the impression that
she had enjoyed it immensely.

Von Uffenbach, although he came to England for the
purpose of continuing his studies as an antiquary, had
a great deal of curiosity and sampled most of the amusements London and its environs had to offer. He visited
the *Folly*, a large ferry-boat moored on the Surrey side of
the Thames, which served as a tavern and a bawdy-house,
with a balcony on the top deck and curtained cabins
below that were 'perfectly secluded'. And he went to the
near-by Cuper's or Cupid's Gardens to stroll among the
groves of trees, where the ladies of the town in all their
finery tempted the unwary to disappear with them into the
bosky undergrowth. He saw a girl dancing on a barrel to
the accompaniment of whirling swords, a performing ape
dressed in a silk coat and breeches, and a Scotsman breaking glasses by shouting at them; and when he went to the
races at Epsom, he was intrigued by the vast crowds of
people he saw there of all classes, especially by the
women riding towards the race-course in companies of
ten or a dozen, dressed in what he thought were men's
clothes and feathered hats. 'One is astonished at the
tumult and the hubbub made by the English on these
occasions,' he wrote. 'There is such a monstrous chasing
about inside the posts, that it makes one quite dizzy.' But
he thought horse-racing was an uncommonly fine sport;
the jockeys looked very smart, 'and it is not easy to
imagine the speed of these horses,' he added, 'for they do
not run, but fly as it were; their stride is so tremendous
that from afar off it looks as though their bellies were on
the ground.'

He was not so keen on bull-baiting, 'an English sport
which vastly delights this nation', though it seemed to

him 'nothing very special'—and his verdict on cock-fighting was much the same. 'It is a sport peculiar to the English, which appears to foreigners very foolish in spite of the pleasure this people takes in it,' he declared, though he found his evening at the Cockpit in Gray's Inn much more diverting when he ventured to gamble a few shillings on the fight. 'The people act like madmen and go on raising the odds to twenty guineas or more,' he remarked, 'and as soon as the cocks appear, the shouting grows even louder. When they are released, some attack, while others run away . . . and impelled by terror, jump down among the people; they are then, however, driven back on the table with great yells and thrust at each other until they get angry. Then it is amazing to see how they peck at each other and especially how they hack with their spurs.' Equally amazing to this perceptive young German was the fact that 'those who put their money on the losing cock have to pay immediately, so that an hostler in his apron often wins several guineas from a Lord; while if a man has made a bet and is unable to pay, for a punishment he is made to sit in a basket fastened to the ceiling and is drawn up in it amidst peals of laughter.'

The Englishman's sense of humour was often incomprehensible to a foreigner, and no wonder; for savage and horrible exhibitions of human indignity made him laugh immoderately. Bedlam was one of the sights of London not to be missed and the lewd antics of the poor lunatics which could be viewed for 2d, were considered to be vastly amusing. The hospital, erected in 1675, was a splendid building on the outside and the intentions of the governors were of the best. Each inmate was supposed to have 'a Room in a good Air, proper Physick and a Diet of boyled Beef, Mutton or Veal and Broth three days a week with Bread and Cheese, Fermity or other Pottage on the remaining four days of the week'. In practice, however, both male and female patients were contained behind bars

like animals in a cage with some filthy straw to lie on, and
there was 'such a rattling of Chains, drumming of Doors,
Ranting, Hallowing and Singing among them, it seemed
as if the Damned had broke loose and put Hell in an
Uproar'. Even Dr Johnson went to have a look at some
of the inmates on two occasions, though he did not find
them funny; he suffered too much from his fear of the
melancholia which he once said had made him mad all his
life 'or at least not sober'.

But Johnson approved of the other horrible exhibition
that pleased the public even more than Bedlam, for when
the hangings at Tyburn were at last done away with in
1783, he was appalled. 'Even Tyburn itself is not safe
from the fury of innovation,' he grumbled. 'Executions
are intended to draw spectators. If they do not draw
spectators, they don't answer their purpose. The old
method was most satisfactory to all parties; the public
was gratified by a procession; the criminal was supported
by it. Why is all this to be swept away?' Being old by then
and prejudiced in favour of the past, he truly believed that
the sight of the condemned men and women bundled
together in carts acted as a deterrent against crime, when,
in fact, it did nothing of the kind; for the processions
from Newgate all the way through Holborn to the gallows
just north of Hyde Park were a Roman holiday for the
shouting, jeering and yelling mob and a sop to their
orgiastic emotions.

Some of the better-class criminals went by coach,
stopping at the Blue Boar in Holborn for their last sup of
burnt brandy, and were dressed in their best clothes. Lord
Ferrers, condemned for murdering his land-steward in
a fit of fury, wore his wedding clothes. Jack Rann,
the highwayman, known as 'Sixteen String Jack' from
the number of ribbons he tied to his breeches to denote the
number of times he had evaded the law, wore white
gloves and a silk brocaded coat, and was the hero of the

F

hour. If the condemned died like gentlemen with a nonchalant swagger, the crowd was satisfied; if they showed fear or spent too long at their prayers, everyone began to bawl and shriek with derisive laughter.

And it was not only the rabble who enjoyed the fun. When James Maclean was taken and condemned soon after he had shot at Horace Walpole in Hyde Park, more than a thousand people visited him in his cell at Newgate and he is said to have fainted twice from the heat and the pressure of the crowd. Among the ladies present on such occasions were two of Horace Walpole's friends, both considered to be great beauties: Miss Ashe, 'a very saucy young lady rumoured to be of very high parentage', and Lady Caroline Petersham, a daughter of the Duke of Grafton. They and their fashionable friends booked seats at high prices in the windows overlooking the processional route or in the stands erected near the gallows and strolled along after breakfast to watch their favourite victims kicking their lives away when the hangman's noose was round their necks and the cart driven away from under their feet. Why go to the playhouse when such amusing entertainment was to be had in the streets?

5

REFINED ENTERTAINMENT

HORACE WALPOLE HIMSELF never confused violence and debauchery with entertainment. He loved pleasure, rising at noon, dining at four and dancing into the early hours of the morning, but he was too refined in his tastes, perhaps too effeminate, ever to enjoy the heavy drinking, excessive gambling and whoring of so many of his aristocratic friends. Even as a schoolboy at Eton he had little inclination for the brutal games and fights of the other boys, and when he set off on the Grand Tour with Thomas Gray, although not as studious as the poet, he was already a fastidious young man. 'You figure us in a set of pleasures, which believe me we do not find,' he wrote from Paris to his friend Richard West. 'Cards and eating are so universal that they absorb all variations of pleasures. The operas, indeed, are much frequented three times a week; but to me they would be a greater penance than eating maigre; their music resembles a goosebery tart as much as it does harmony.' The grandeurs of Versailles did not excite his admiration either. He thought the great front 'a lumber of littleness, composed of black brick stuck full of bad old busts' and the garden, 'littered with statues and fountains and avenues of waterpots squirting up cascadelins, a garden for a great child'.

Travelling on to Italy across the Alps was much more impressive and very terrifying. At the foot of Mount Cenis, they were obliged to quit their chaise, which was taken to pieces and loaded on to mules, and to be carried in low arm-chairs on poles by the savage and quarrelsome alpine porters, who scampered up and down the frozen precipices like wild beasts, with no thought of their passengers' nervous apprehension. Huddled against the cold in beaver bonnets, beaver stockings, muffs and bearskins, they took four days to negotiate the crossing among 'such uncouth rocks and such uncomely inhabitants' as Walpole hoped he would never see again. 'The least slip had tumbled us into such a fog and such an eternity, as we would never have found our way out of again,' he wrote, and although he and Gray escaped without accident, his little dog Tory, 'the prettiest, fattest, dearest little creature', was seized by a wolf and carried off to 'a horrid death'.

Their arrival in Turin brought the travellers back to civilization, which was very welcome; and from there they went on to Genoa, enjoying their leisure and satisfying their curiosity in 'the happy country where huge lemons grow'. They went sightseeing in Bologna and then across the Apennines to Florence to stay with Sir Horace Mann, the British Minister, who entertained them in his own house. Gray continued to pursue his studies with great earnestness, making copious notes in his meticulous handwriting of all the paintings and sculpture of the Renaissance, while Walpole, as the son of Sir Robert, was made a great fuss of by high society, forsaking the serious purpose of his visit for the more frivolous delights of the balls and masquerades. 'I have done nothing but slip out of my domino into bed, and out of bed into my domino,' he

wrote. 'The end of the Carnival is frantic, bacchanalian; all
the morn one makes parties in masque to the shops and
coffee houses, and all the evening to the operas and balls.
Then I have danced, good gods! how I have danced!'

Rome was a disappointment after this. Roman *con-
versazioni* were a dreadful bore and Roman hospitality
altogether very inferior. All the monuments and pictures
appeared to be decayed or decaying—and Naples was no
better. Walpole missed the gaiety of life in Florence. He
bought a bust of Vespasian, some bronze medallions and
other antiquities and hurried back to the Casa Ambrosio
overlooking the Arno, where 'in the serene Italian air one
may linger all night in a dressing-gown, eating iced fruits
to the notes of guitar'. The candles blazed in the great
palazzi of the romantic Tuscan city and the lovely
daughters of Lady Pomfret and the almond-eyed beauties
of the Florentine aristocracy danced to the airy music of
the viols and the harpsichord. All his life Walpole retained
his delight in dancing; but thirty years later when he
looked back to his quarrel with Gray which exploded soon
after they left Florence, he was rather ashamed of being
'too young, too fond of my own diversions, too much
intoxicated by indulgence and vanity' to have given the
more sober qualities of his scholarly friend enough
consideration. They parted from each other with high
words at Reggio, Gray going on to Venice and Walpole
returning home to a political crisis which destroyed his
father's long term of office as Prime Minister.

What could well have been a catastrophe for Sir Robert's
youngest son was mitigated by the fact that Horace had
no political ambition whatever and never sought to
advance his own claims at Court. He preferred a life of
leisure and pleasure in Arlington Street and at Strawberry Hill, the miniature Gothic castle he bought at
Twickenham, where he could pursue his dilettante
interests at his ease. Never extravagant, he enjoyed a

modest income which was quite sufficient for his needs and, as a spectator of the fashionable world from his return to England in 1741 until his death in 1797, he found the follies of those more ambitious than himself endlessly diverting. He knew absolutely everything that was going on, was a shrewd judge of character and events and refined the art of letter-writing to an extraordinary degree of perfection. Always witty, sometimes waspish and unkind in his comments on people and things, he was none the less never deliberately destructive except of pretentiousness and cupidity; and he cultivated a style to entertain his correspondents that was full of brilliant observation, pungency and unexpected irony, describing his pleasures with the fastidious delight of a cat with a dish of cream.

'I am come hither for a few days,' he wrote to Sir Horace Mann from Strawberry Hill in May 1749, 'to repose myself after a torrent of diversions, and am writing to you in my charming bow-window with a tranquillity and satisfaction which, I fear, I am grown old enough [he was thirty-two] to prefer to the hurry of amusements in which the whole world has lived for this past week. We have at last celebrated the Peace [of Aix-la-Chapelle] and that as much in extremes as we generally do everything, whether we have reason to be glad or sorry, pleased or angry. Last Tuesday it was proclaimed; the King did not go to St Paul's, but at night the whole town was illuminated. The next day was what was called "a jubilee-Masquerade in the Venetian manner" at Ranelagh; it had nothing Venetian in it, but was by far the best understood and prettiest spectacle I ever saw. . . . When you entered, you found the whole garden filled with masks and spread with tents, which remained all night *very commodely*. In one quarter was a Maypole dressed with garlands and people dancing round it to a tabor and pipe and rustic music, all masqued, as were all the bands . . . some like huntsmen with French horns, some like peasants, and a troop of harlequins and scaramouches in the little open temple on the mount. On the canal was a sort of gondola, adorned with flags and streamers, and filled with music, rowing about. All round the outside of the amphitheatre were shops, filled with Dresden china, japan etc., and all the shopkeepers in mask. The amphitheatre was illuminated; and in the middle was a circular bower, composed of all kinds of firs in tubs, from twenty to thirty feet high; under them orange-trees, with small lamps in each orange, and below them all sorts of the finest auriculas in pots; and festoons of natural flowers hanging from tree to tree.'

All this picturesque decoration enraptured Walpole. Indeed, Ranelagh Pleasure Gardens, opened in 1742, had 'totally beat Vauxhall' in his opinion. 'Nobody goes anywhere else,' he wrote, 'everyone goes there. . . . You can't see your foot without treading on a Prince of Wales or a Duke of Cumberland.' The gardens were exquisitely laid out with a canal and a series of Arcadian walks and groves, leading off into the grottoes and arbours designed to give privacy to those of the visitors who were amorously inclined. The superb and richly gilded Rotunda, with two tiers of boxes, enclosed a circular promenade hung with splendid chandeliers, and here the very latest and most extravagant fashions of the *beau-monde* could be seen as the company strolled about or retired into the boxes to savour the latest *chronique scandaleuse* over a dish of tea and a plate of thin bread and butter. Concerts were given for their entertainment by the best instrumentalists, by the eight-year-old Mozart in 1764 and by the most celebrated singers of the day. One young lady listening to 'the divine warbling' of the Italian *castrato* Tenducci, thought she had been 'wafted into Paradise', and even Dr Johnson, who did not often look kindly on frivolous things, declared that the *coup d'oeil* of Ranelagh was the finest thing he had ever seen.

Behaviour at Ranelagh was more restrained on the whole than at Vauxhall, the much older Pleasure Gardens which had been renovated in 1732 by Hogarth's friend, Jonathen Tyers. According to one French visitor, Ranelagh was really rather dull. '*On s'ennui avec de la mauvaise musique, du thé et du beurre,*' he commented, and certainly at Vauxhall the refreshments were more exciting. Supper after the concerts consisted of chicken and ham or a dish of powdered beef, with fruit tarts, custards, cheese-cakes and syllabubs laced with wine; and there was Arrack punch at 8s a bowl and the special Vauxhall Nectar, a potent mixture of rum and syrup 'with an addition of benzoic acid or the flowers of benjamin'.

It was possible also to have fun taking a picnic to Vauxhall. Horace Walpole joined a very gay party in the summer of 1750, travelling there by barge with a boat-load of French horns in attendance. Lady Caroline Petersham had invited all her friends: the lovely little Miss Ashe, a pretty Miss Beauclerc, a very foolish Miss Sparre, the Duke of Kingston, Lord March, Harry Vane and Lord Granby, who came on to the Pleasure Gardens from Jenny's Whim, a tavern in Chelsea, where he had already been drinking champagne and playing Brag with a number of other ladies and gentlemen of rank and fashion. With a great deal of merriment and some badinage between the hiccuping Lord Granby and the foolish Miss Sparre, 'at last we assembled in our booth', Walpole wrote, 'Lady Caroline in the front, with the vizor of her hat erect, and looking gloriously jolly and handsome. She had fetched my brother Orford from the next box, where he was enjoying himself with his *petite partie*, to help us mince chickens. We minced seven chickens into a china dish, which Lady Caroline stewed over a lamp with three pats of butter and a flagon of water, stirring and rattling, and laughing, and we every minute expecting to have the dish fly about our ears. She had brought Betty, the fruit-girl from St James's Street with hampers of strawberries and cherries from Rogers's, and made her wait upon us, and then made her sup by us at a little table. The conversation was no less lively than the whole transaction. . . . In short, the whole air of our party was sufficient as you may easily imagine, to take up the whole attention of the garden; so much so that we had the whole concourse round our booth . . . till Harry Vane took up a bumper, and drank their healths. . . . It was three o'clock before we got home.'

Lady Caroline, married to a sulky and eccentric husband, was one of Walpole's most treasured friends. Apparently he never seriously considered marrying anyone or taking a mistress, but he adored the society of pretty, intelligent young women with whom he could frisk about happily in the guise of a good-natured bachelor uncle. A superb raconteur, he maintained a teasing, sprightly attitude towards them, entertaining them with his witty anecdotes spiced with a good deal of well-bred malice, yet praising the looks and the vivacity of those he was fond of with genuine sincerity. He loved his young niece Maria, who had 'the sweetest delicacy in the world', and General Conway's gifted daughter Mrs Damer, one of the first women ever to work as a sculptor; and he built a special closet at Strawberry Hill, hung with Indian blue damask, to show off the 'seven incomparable drawings in soot-water' done by his beloved Lady Di Beauclerk, somewhat over-estimating her rather slender talent as an artist. Playing at cards and gambling did not amuse him; he preferred gossiping for hours on end with his young and his older friends, the Countess of Suffolk, Lady Hervey and the Countess of Ossory, recalling the scandals and the intrigues of the past from his great store of memories and dressing them up in new clothes to divert his audience.

Every other year from 1765 to 1771, he went to Paris to visit old Madame du Deffand, the ex-mistress of the

Duke of Orleans, who was over seventy when Walpole first met her and totally blind, but whose amazing vitality kept her out and about until three o'clock in the morning, and every week until her death in 1780, he wrote her a long letter. Then, when it seemed as if life was draining away from Horace himself and the pain of his gout at last made him give up dancing, he met two girls in their twenties, Miss Mary and Miss Agnes Berry, 'the best informed and the most perfect creatures I ever saw at that age . . . Mary, the eldest, sweet, with fine dark eyes, that are very lively when she speaks, with a symmetry of face that is more interesting from being pale; Agnes, the younger, with an agreeable countenance, hardly to be called handsome, but almost.' They were not well off—their father had been disinherited on marrying for love and was now a widower; and when Walpole persuaded them to move into a cottage on his Twickenham estate, the scandalmongers in the neighbourhood attributed their response to his pleasure in their company to dishonourable motives. He at once denied this slur on their integrity and reaffirmed his affection for them in a letter to the Countess of Ossory. 'I am proud of my partiality for my "two wives",' he wrote, 'and since the ridicule can only fall on me and not on them, I care not a straw for its being said that I am in love with one of them—people shall choose which: it is as much with both as either, and I am infinitely too old to regard the *qu'en dit on*.'

Strawberry Hill was finished at last. Against the prevailing taste for classicism, Walpole had put all his instinctive love of the picturesque into his little Gothic castle, collecting stained-glass windows from the neglected English cathedrals and churches and building a Gothic staircase, a Round Chamber, a refectory and a gallery for his paintings, his bric-à-brac and his antique busts. 'I did not mean to make my house so Gothic as to exclude convenience and modern refinements in luxury,' he declared. 'It was built to please my own taste and in some degree to realize my own visions'—and as such, it was unique. Visitors arrived from all over the country and from abroad to see what he had done, many of them strangers, and were shown round by the housekeeper while Walpole went into hiding in his own bedchamber; and from time to time he gave breakfast parties and supper parties for his friends, hiring musicians to entertain them with sweet melodies on 'the French horns and clarionettes'. But he was equally content alone there among his odds and ends of virtu and his goldfish, pottering about the garden, attending to his private printing-press and writing—for ever writing the brilliant, witty and scintillating letters which gave so much pleasure to his recipients and expressed every nuance of his feelings from the most frivolous personal incident to the grim events of the American War and the French Revolution.

Town bred and a town bird, Horace Walpole had little use for country life aside from his own small reflection of it at Twickenham. He enjoyed visiting the great parks and gardens of his noble friends, examining and criticizing the architecture of their houses and acting as a connoisseur of their paintings and manuscripts. But he hated riding and despised their love of sport, and found the average squire 'a mountain of roast beef' and a great bore. 'I see no difference between a country gentleman and a sirloin,' he wrote. 'Whenever the first laughs or the latter is cut, there run out just the same streams of gravy.... They tire me, they fatigue me; I don't know what to do with them. ... Indeed I find this fatigue worse in the country than in town, because there one can avoid it and has more resources.'

Without an ardent love of horses and hounds, and a gargantuan appetite for beef and ale, there was certainly no means of avoiding boredom in the country, except for the wealthy landowners who could indulge in their passion for glorifying their houses and gardens. Such refinements were beyond the intellect and the purse of the great majority of the squires, who farmed their own land and were content to jog along with no more mental effort than was demanded of them on the local bench as justices of the peace. Many of them spoke the broadest provincial dialect in common with the yeomen farmers and were only to be distinguished from them by the possession of a few more acres, a family coat of arms, a manor house and the respect due to them as gentlemen. They were broad shouldered, tough and horsy, with boorish manners, high blood-pressure and a contempt for everything un-English; much addicted to the bottle and the chase, to snaring and shooting game and going to bed with the pretty maidens in the village, while their own wives and daughters for the want of a coach had to amuse themselves at home, playing at cards or making black-currant jelly.

Fielding's Squire Western in *Tom Jones*, whose thoughts were confined to 'the field, the stable or the dog-kennel' and who declared loudly that Tom was none the worse for getting a bastard in the village, was no caricature. Bellicose, greedy, rank with sweat and drunk every day after dinner, he was, none the less, never dishonest in his lust for life and he loved his daughter with a blundering awkward tenderness that brought him to tears of rage and impotence. Sophia's accomplishments, her playing on the harpsichord, her beauty and her modesty were perhaps exaggerated for the novelist's own purpose, for women had little opportunity to develop a gracious kind of life in the first half of the century. They lived in the most shocking isolation. In the winter they seldom went abroad at all, except in their own village. Travelling, either riding pillion behind their husbands or in the family coach if there was one, was dangerous and difficult. The roads were deep in mud and often impassable. Visiting

one's neighbours for any kind of jollification meant
spending the night with them, or several nights if the
weather turned bad. Even going as far as the nearest
market town was an expedition to be viewed with some
apprehension, though every town, large or small, as the
prosperity of the country increased, began to build
Assembly Rooms to provide entertainment for the county
families living in the district and the squires who could
not afford to bring their marriageable daughters to
London, took them there instead.

Anyone used to London society naturally found the
company at these local, provincial assemblies very suspect.
Mrs Pendarves did not think anything of Gloucester,
where her mother and sister were living to save expense.
'It affords so little variety that I can send you no accounts
from hence worthy your notice,' she wrote to her friend
Lady Throckmorton. 'We have assemblies once a week,
such as they are, and we go because we would not be
thought churlish. They are made up of an odd mixture
and if my sister and myself loved pulling people to pieces,
we should find material enough to exercise our wits upon
—at least excellent food for ill-nature.'

Mrs Pendarves was perhaps not quite so good-natured
as she pretended to be, but she was not a snob according
to the standards of the eighteenth century. She was a
Granville and a niece of Lord Lansdowne, and if she
frowned on the mixed company at Gloucester, it was
simply because she was born with the aristocratic
prejudice of her time, which did not admit merchants and
middle-class folk to the upper reaches of society unless
they were so rich that they could buy estates for themselves
and acquire a title. She was, moreover, a poor relation of
the Granvilles and had already suffered from their high-
bred attitude of long-established superiority, being far too
ladylike and much too obedient to object when her Uncle
Lansdowne had married her off at the age of seventeen to

an old and gouty friend of his, Alexander Pendarves, who turned out to be a drunken brute with a ferociously jealous disposition. Thrust away in his isolated Cornish castle, 'built of ugly coarse stone and propt with two great stone buttresses, covered in moss and mould', she had heroically made the best of a lamentable bargain until seven years later, when she was happily released by the sudden death of her unpleasant spouse.

As an attractive young widow, living again in the best society and on very intimate terms with the Duchess of Portland and her family, she was in no hurry to marry again. Once was enough, perhaps. 'Moneyed men are covetous, disagreeable wretches,' she wrote, 'fine men with little estates are coxcombs; those of real merit are seldom to be found. . . . As for your rural squires I detest them and your town fops are my abomination.' She prided herself greatly on her virtue and her independence, disliked 'the ogling and tweezing and whispering and glancing' at Court, where there was 'no laughing and dancing, only standing and walking and fine ladies' airs', and frequently retired into the country with the Duchess of Portland to enjoy 'the gentle delights of Bulstrode' and to work at her knotting, her cherry-netting, her festoons of shells and her painting 'between the coolings of her tea'.

People admired her artistic taste which she had leisure enough to develop with great assiduity. Mrs Montagu, that tireless, vivacious and often very tiresome young woman, soon to become the leader of the blue-stocking ladies who preferred conversation to cards as a way of showing off their glittering intellectual abilities, 'epistolized' her in the flowery and high-flown language she was in the habit of using. 'To a *mind* that *comprehends* you have a *hand that records* and represents its beauties,' she wrote. 'Your drawing-room boasts of eternal spring and nature blooms there when it languishes in gardens; and not only the prospects and landscapes are represented by your art, but even human passions and fugitive thoughts are expressed and fixed by the strokes of your pencil.' And this was not all—for everyone admired her refinement of character, her charm and her sensibility; her friends and her family receiving the long letters she wrote to them with raptures of delight and infinite protestations of affection and goodwill. To her friend Mrs Donellan, she was a paragon, 'the agreeableness of her manners, the polite-ness of her behaviour and the winning grace in all her words and actions' unparalleled, 'her innate modesty and discerning judgment' never at fault. So it was all the more surprising and to the Granvilles downright shocking when, after nineteen years of widowhood, she suddenly decided to marry an elderly Irish widower with no blue blood in his veins at all.

Dr Delany was a clergyman and a friend of Dean Swift's. Though several years older than his bride, he was still very sprightly, with a pink face and a charming manner. His courtship was discreet and when Mary Pendarves yielded to the sincerity of his devotion, she was not mistaken in his qualities as a man of 'real merit'. With a great deal of special pleading and self-justification, she persuaded the Granvilles to accept him—all except her brother who refused to be reconciled to her marriage with a commoner; and using her influence with the Duke of Devonshire, she managed to get her new husband appointed to the vacant deanery of Down. She was now a woman of forty-three with a mind of her own, willing to outface the charge of marrying beneath her, and she knew she had chosen wisely. Writing from her new home in Ireland, she expressed her great delight in Dr Delany's 'sweet dwelling' at Delville, in the splendid view of Dublin harbour from her parlour windows and in the garden, where she set about making a shell grotto and found many 'private seats with lovely prospects' where she and the Dean could rest and converse on summer evenings.

They kept 'a simple table', she wrote, though the menu she copied out for her sister's edification and amusement consisted of glazed turkey, boiled neck of mutton, soup, plum pudding, roast loin of veal and venison pasty for the first course, and partridges, sweetbreads, collared pig, creamed apple-tart, crabs, fricassee of eggs and pigeons for the second—and this apparently was just an ordinary dinner for one or two guests. From five o'clock until nine she sometimes entertained the Dean's relations and friends with dancing, followed by a cold collation with tea and coffee, and the dear Dean 'seemed as well pleased with looking on' as everyone else was with the dancing. His niece was 'very lively and good-humoured and very ready to assist', his friend Mr Ford 'a worthy sort of person' and Mrs Hamilton's son was 'a very sober, well-behaved youth'. In fact, society at Delville was modest, circumspect and confined within the bounds of religion and decorum; there was no gambling, no drinking or eating to excess, in spite of the crabs and the collared pig.

Things were very different in Dublin, where the Lord-Lieutenant, always an English peer, held Court at the Castle in great state with a magnificence that was often a little vulgar. 'The great folks at the Castle continue to show us great favour,' Mrs Delany wrote, 'but we pay them little attendance, no more than not to be remarked as backward'; and again, rather piously: 'This Winter everybody is engaged in a more public way of diverting themselves, but I have withdrawn myself from these sort of entertainments and find more pleasure in the quiet enjoyment of my own amusements at home than a crowd can give me. It is very happy that as our season of life changes our taste for pleasures alter. In the spring and summer of life we *flutter and bask* in the sunshine of diversions . . . in the autumn [she was forty-five] and winter of life we by degrees seek for shade and shelter, and if we have made a good and prudent gathering of fruit and harvest, we may then have a full enjoyment of them, as long as the great Author and Giver thinks fit.'

These edifying sentiments of Mrs Delany's were the basis of her philosophy to the very end of her long life forty-five years later, but few people in Dublin at this time would have been willing to agree with them; for the Irish city shared with London its extremes of poverty and opulence, of mob violence, raffish gaiety and privilege, and the contrasts, if anything, were even worse: English rule and Irish resentment were always on the verge of explosion. The Court of the Lord-Lieutenant was, however, more amusing and more splendid than that of his master King George, and the manœuvring for desirable places in it a never-ending source of the scandalous and malicious gossip that high society found so entertaining. Younger sons of the English nobility were sent there to sow their wild oats, young ladies without a sufficient dowry to sell themselves in the London marriage-market, packed off with a chaperon to try their luck with the Irish aristocracy, and the routs at the Castle were as crowded as the drawing-rooms at St James's. There were balls and concerts and banquets of great extravagance and, outside the capital, all the pleasures of hunting and horse-racing, shooting and fishing in the green leisure of the countryside.

Irish horses and Irish country houses were lively and elegant, Irish hospitality was open-handed and irresistible; and the intellectual entertainment in Dublin was in no way inferior to London. Handel's visit to the city in the winter of 1741-2 offered the Irish nobility and gentry a series of oratorio performances by subscription, which excited an enormous amount of enthusiasm. The first concert was 'crowded with a more numerous and polite Audience than ever was seen upon the like Occasion . . .

and to show their Taste for all Kinds of Genius, they gave
all imaginable Encouragements to this grand Musick.'
Four months later the first performance of *The Messiah* in
the Fishamble Street Musick Hall, designed to hold 600
people, was even more of a sensation. Ladies were requested to abandon their hoops and gentlemen their
swords so that room could be made available for another
hundred persons, and the *Dublin Journal* reported: 'Words
are wanting to express the exquisite Delight this Sacred
Grand Oratorio afforded to the admiring crouded
Audience. The Sublime, the Grand and the Tender,
adapted to the most elevated, majestick and moving
Words, conspired to transport and charm the ravished
Heart and Ear.' Handel himself, having suffered a decline
in popularity in London, was delighted with his success
and with Susannah Cibber, a sister of Thomas Arne's and
the distressed wife of Colley Cibber's despicable son
Theophilus, who sang the mezzo-soprano arias in *The
Messiah* with such feeling that at one performance Dr
Delany, unable to restrain his emotion, is said to have
started up in his seat and to have cried out in a loud voice:
'Woman! thy sins be forgiven thee!'

Poor Susannah was in need of the Dean's absolution.
Having established herself in London as an actress, she
had only just ventured to reappear on the stage in Dublin
after her vicious husband had brought two legal actions
against her lover, Mr Sloper, to whom he had in reality
sold his wife 'to supply his own pecuniary wants'. Once
when Susannah was in hiding with Mr Sloper at Burnham
in Buckinghamshire, Theophilus had stormed into her
bedchamber, seized all her jewellery and carried her off,
still in her nightgown, to a waiting coach, which drove
through the night to London. He then got Mr Stint, a
candle-snuffer at the playhouse, to keep her locked up in a
room without a fire at the Bull's Head Tavern in Clare
Market and was only robbed of his victim when her

brother, Thomas Arne, arrived with a case of pistols and a number of sturdy friends to break down the door and set her free.

By this time, 'having no further expectations from Mr Sloper's generosity, Theophilus was determined to try whether he could not obtain by means of the law some compensation for the injury he affected to feel'. Luckily the judge and the jury were not so easily taken in as he supposed. Even the evidence of Mrs Hayes, a lodging-house keeper in Leicester Fields, who admitted to spying through a hole which her husband had bored in the wainscot and said she could 'see Mr Sloper and Mrs Cibber very plain when he kissed her and took her on his lap', did not carry much weight, for it was obvious to everyone that Cibber himself had thrown his wife into Mr Sloper's arms more for what he could get out of it than for her own pleasure. Mr Sloper was foolish enough 'to walk abroad in his slippers and in an undress' at Burnham, which proved his guilt, but he was immensely kind to the dis-traught Susannah, who maintained her dignity to the very end of the whole unhappy business. She could not, however, act again at Drury Lane while her depraved husband still had a share in the management, so after retiring into the country for a year or two with Mr Sloper, she went to Dublin instead, where her grace and her beauty enraptured a new audience more than willing to forgive her transgressions.

There were two theatres in Dublin: the New Theatre in Smock Alley, which had been rebuilt in 1734 and the Theatre Royal in Aungier Street. Both were more com-modious for the nobility and gentry than Drury Lane or Covent Garden, as they provided 'box rooms' or large, finely decorated saloons outside the private boxes, where patrons could meet to gossip and quiz each other until their chairs or their carriages arrived to carry them home. The congestion in Smock Alley was notorious on a popular night as the street was very narrow and the Irish coachmen and chairmen fought a running battle with each other for priority. Ladies in long brocaded gowns were liable to be pushed to the wall or doused in mud unless they picked their way with care, and the more raffish elements of the audience issuing from the gallery, enjoyed their discomfiture as much as the performance they had paid to see. But the Irish audience was a very intelligent one and highly critical—nothing short of the best was good enough; and the Irish theatre was a forcing-house of talent. Wilks started there, so did Macklin, Thomas Sheridan, Woodward, Mossop and Spranger Barry, the handsome son of a Dublin silversmith, with a refined air of melancholy, a melting voice and a tall, aristocratic figure. Old Quin was a frequent visitor and Garrick, immediately after his first brilliant season in London at the theatre in Goodman's Fields, accepted an invitation to go there in 1742. He travelled to Chester in a post-chaise and boarded the packet for Dublin with Signora Barbarini, the ballerina, and Peg Woffington, who was then 'in the bloom of youth, possessed of a fine figure, great beauty and every elegant accomplishment'.

'Lovely Peggy' was going home to the city where she had walked the streets as a child selling watercress and where, it is said, she was seen by the celebrated French rope-dancer Madame Violante, who was performing in a booth theatre near the College Green. Madame Violante promptly took the barefoot child from her destitute mother into her company of 'Lilliputians', taught her how to act and sing and cast her at the age of ten as Polly in *The Beggar's Opera*, then as Macheath when the 'Lilliputians' arrived at the Little Theatre in the Haymarket in 1732. After this nothing more was heard of her until she reappeared at the Aungier Street Theatre in Dublin in the winter of 1739–40 and startled everyone by playing Sir Harry Wildair in *The Constant Couple*. No woman had ever

dared to act this part written for a man and made famous
by Wilks, but no man—not even Garrick—was ever liked
in it again while Woffington was alive. She had splendid,
impudent Irish eyes, a brilliant smile and great fascination,
and was quite without the vanity that was to be expected
from such an accomplished actress. Returning to London
after her success in Dublin, she forced her way into John
Rich's private residence in Bloomsbury while he was
drinking tea and eating toast surrounded by all of his
twenty-seven cats, and so charmed him that he gave her an
immediate engagement at Covent Garden. Soon the whole
town was talking about her—and talking kindly, for she
was generous and warm-hearted as well as beautiful and
talented. 'Her conversation was in a stile of elegance,
always pleasing and often instructive. She abounded in
wit and her understanding was superior to the generality
of her sex', one writer declared, adding rather sententiously:
'Forgive her one female error, and it may fairly be said
that she was adorned with every virtue.'

Her one female error was not to be wondered at,
considering how hotly she was pursued by the opposite
sex. In fact, the faithless younger son of an Irish peer was
rumoured to have broken her heart when she was very
young and while every male seen in her company—even
old Colley Cibber and his still more ancient crony, Owen
McSwinney—was said at one time or another to have
enjoyed more than her friendship, Peg Woffington was
not so easily won. She was at her best among men:
'Women,' she said, 'talk nothing but silks and scandal';
but she held her admirers off with a tantalizing independence, and when Garrick went to Ireland with her, he
was not yet her lover, though he was deeply in love.

He was twenty-five, quick and attractive, flushed with
his first high success as an actor, not yet encumbered with
the responsibilities of managing a theatre and free to
choose a mistress or a wife. He wanted both—he wanted

Peg; and within a week or two of their arrival, one half
of his desire was fulfilled. But he still wanted marriage:

> If Truth can fix thy wav'ring heart,
>   Let Damon urge his claim;
> He feels the passion void of art,
>   The pure, the constant flame.
>
> Though sighing swains their torments tell,
>   Their sensual love contemn;
> They only prize the beauteous shell,
>   But slight the inward gem.
>
> Possession cures the wounded heart,
>   Destroys the transient fire;
> But when the mind receives the dart,
>   Enjoyment whets desire.

Garrick was no fool. He knew the theatre well enough
and he knew Peg's reputation. But he believed he was
more constant than any of her other suitors, even the rich
and fashionable Sir Charles Hanbury-Williams and the
still more dangerous Lord Darnley. And they were young
and in love. It seemed as though their Irish summer of
delight might go on for ever, not end—as it did three
years later—in a terrible quarrel, which Garrick was never
to forget and which none of his friends ever dared to
mention to him, even after he had achieved a happy
marriage with a Viennese danseuse known as La Violette.
Lovely Peggy continued to act with him—she was
indispensable; but they conducted their business on the
stage through a third party, without ever speaking a single
intimate word to each other again.

6

INTELLECTUAL PLEASURES

DAVID GARRICK AND Samuel Johnson had travelled to London together in 1737. They could not afford the public coach or the stage-wagon; they 'rode and tied' with one horse between them, entertaining themselves on the way by reciting poetry. Garrick had 1½d in his pocket when they arrived, Johnson exactly 2½d. Both were born of respectable middle-class parents living in genteel poverty. Garrick's grandfather was a Huguenot refugee, his father a Captain in the Dragoons on half-pay and his mother the daughter of a vicar-choral of the superb cathedral which dominated Lichfield. Johnson was the son of an elderly, unbusinesslike bookseller, whose house stood in the market-square. He was born in 1709, 'a poor deseased infant, almost blind, infected with scrofula and deaf in one ear', and had grown into an exceedingly uncouth young man with a pock-marked face as pallid as a lump of suet, and a nervous disease that made him twitch all over and roll himself about in convulsive fits. He was nine years older than Garrick, who had once been his pupil, but whereas the boy David by 1742 was earning

£500 a year at Drury Lane and being fêted by high society, the goliath Samuel was still dining on bread, meat and water at a tavern in the Strand or going without his dinner altogether.

It says much for the fundamental courage and generosity of Johnson's character that he was not more embittered by his young friend's spectacular success. He had failed utterly through no fault of his own. His home was unhappy and his days at Lichfield Grammar School tormented by the brutal flogging of the headmaster. He was short-sighted, indolent and clumsy; and at Oxford, though his friends considered him 'a gay and frolicsome' undergraduate, it was in reality 'bitterness that they mistook for frolic', he declared later, adding: 'I was rude and violent. I was miserably poor and I thought to fight my way by my literature and my wit.' He left without a degree, with no money and no prospects, a victim of his own terrible moods of depression and condemned to lead the life of a third-rate provincial schoolmaster eating his heart out in despair. Looking for comfort and consolation, he married a widow from Birmingham and although he always maintained that it was a love-match on both sides, poor Tetty, as he called her, lost all of her fortune amounting to some £600 in his misguided attempt to open an academy for young gentlemen at Edial near Lichfield. The young gentlemen, including Garrick, enjoyed themselves peeping through the keyhole into their master's bedroom to watch 'his tumultuous and awkward fondness' for his spouse, without otherwise improving their education.

So Johnson had set out for London at the age of twenty-eight to try his luck with a tragedy and with a letter from Mr Walmesley, a worthy citizen of Lichfield, recommending him as 'a very good scholar and poet'. The tragedy, called *Irene*, was written in blank verse and failed to attract the attention of Mr Fleetwood, the manager of

Drury Lane. Grub Street, the sordid grave of so many
ambitious young poets, offered the only alternative means
of earning a few guineas. It had not changed much since
the time of Queen Elizabeth. The old, half-timbered
houses in Moorfields were rotting away; want and necessity hounded the wretched, ragged writers who forgathered in the sleazy taverns to entertain themselves with
drinking when they could find the money or someone to
treat them. But Johnson had courage and he found a
friend in Edward Cave, the shrewd editor and founder of
the *Gentleman's Magazine,* who lived in the ancient gateway
to the Hospital of the Knights of St John of Jerusalem
in Clerkenwell. Cave recognized his abilities, tactfully
allowed him to hide behind a screen to conceal his
shabbiness when there were other visitors to St John's
Lodge and paid him ten guineas for his poem on London.

This, an 'Imitation' of Juvenal's third satire, was a
distillation of Johnson's own experience in the capital and
of the love-hate relationship to it which was to dominate
the rest of his life. So far he had known only poverty and
frustration and the horror of provoking derision by his
eccentric appearance. A lesser character could well have
been destroyed by the misery and the humiliation he
suffered. Yet his resilience was the one thing—perhaps the
only thing at this time—that never failed him; and London
with its splendour and its corruption, its excitement and
its squalor, stimulated his imagination in a way that his
provincial home could never have equalled, besides increasing his compassion for its victims. Pleasure was not
entirely lacking either in spite of his circumstances, for he
had a great capacity for enjoyment when his melancholia
lifted and he made new friends among the Grub Street
writers. He helped the impecunious Samuel Boyse to get
his clothes out of pawn and loved him for rashly spending
his last half-guinea on mushrooms and truffles to eat with
his meat, so that afterwards he again had to pawn his shirt

and retire to bed under a blanket which had so many holes in it that he was able to continue writing his copy through them. He loved a rogue called Henry Hervey, who was kind to him, frequently inviting him to dinner when he was hungry; and in Richard Savage, a dissolute poet twelve years older than himself, he found an intimate companion for his nights and days in the restless, teeming city.

Savage claimed to be the bastard son of the Countess of Macclesfield and Earl Rivers and to have been most cruelly persecuted by his mother. He was a wild and fascinating creature, living by his wits on the charity of his friends, a paranoic bent on self-destruction and quite incapable of learning by experience to conduct his life into less turbulent waters. At one time when he received an allowance of £200 a year from his mother's cousin, Lord Tyrconnel, 'his appearance was splendid, his expenses large and his acquaintance extensive. He was courted by all who endeavoured to be thought men of genius and caressed by all who valued themselves upon a refined taste. . . . His presence was sufficient to make any place of public entertainment popular; and his approbation and example constituted the fashion.' Before long, however, he had quarrelled with Lord Tyrconnel, and 'his intemperate desire for pleasure and habitual slavery to his passions involved him in many perplexities. . . . So much was he delighted with wine and conversation, and so long had he been accustomed to live by chance, that he would at any time go into a tavern without scruple, and trust for the reckoning to the liberality of the company he found there. . . . His conversation was so entertaining and his address so pleasing, that few thought the pleasure which they received from him dearly purchased by paying for his wine.'

While the moralist in Johnson disapproved of this irresponsible behaviour, the rebellious Bohemian instinct in him admired it and was enthralled. When neither could afford a lodging for the night, they roamed the streets together with a cheerfulness the young man from the provinces never forgot. Savage was a master of the art of conversation and never 'the first of the company that desired to separate'. In him the despised scholar from Lichfield found a mind as brilliant and as lively as his own; through him he discovered his own compulsive delight in talking the sky down. Indeed, such conversation with the sharp sword-play of unexpected wit and argument, the sudden hit, the high defence of a wild idea tossed into the air and beaten into shape through the mind and the imagination and the exact significance of a word—such talk intoxicated Johnson. It was meat and drink to his soul; it gave him freedom from the harsh necessity of earning his living as a literary hack, freedom from the drudgery, the frustration and the failure that had dogged him for so long and a powerful sense of his own inexhaustible intellectual capacity. In company and in conversation he was to become a giant, riding above his ugliness, his disabilities and his inhibitions, though not yet, not for another twenty years.

In 1739 Savage parted from him with tears in his eyes, 'furnished with fifteen guineas' for his journey by the generosity of his friends, who promised him a further sum on condition that he retired to Swansea to devote himself to literature. Of course, he did nothing of the kind. He got as far as Bristol, quickly exhausted the hospitality of the merchants there, who at first found him very gay and amusing, and was finally put into prison for debt. Mr Dagg, the keeper of the prison, was uncommonly kind to him, inviting him to his table 'without any certainty of recompense' and allowing him to receive visitors. 'But sometimes he descended to lower amusements and diverted himself in the kitchen with the conversation of criminals, for it was not pleasing for him to be much

without company.' Then suddenly, he was seized with a
violent pain in his back and in a day or two was dead.
Johnson at once threw off his habitual lethargy and with
great speed wrote an account of his life, pouring into it
much of his own feeling and creating a vivid, sardonic
picture of their common experience in the desperate hand-
to-mouth existence of Grub Street. While he made no
attempt to conceal his friend's vices, he comprehended
them with a humane and charitable fellow-feeling, and the
result was the most moving biography that had yet been
written in the English language. It was published
anonymously in 1744 and Johnson got fifteen guineas for
it, twelve of which he already owed to friends in Lichfield;
but it was a turning-point in his career.

Two years later a group of publishers commissioned
him to write a new *Dictionary of the English Language* and
he moved into a house in Gough Square with room for
six assistants. The plan of the work was dedicated to that
cynical and elegant nobleman the Earl of Chesterfield, who
gave him ten guineas and then forgot all about it, having
no idea of the labour involved and little sympathy with
the author, whose progress was slow and difficult and
bedevilled by the disastrous decline in his wife's physical
and mental health. Poor Tetty had taken to drink and
drugs, to painting her swollen cheeks a florid red and to
dressing herself up in fantastic colours; she refused to let
her husband share her bed and spent most of her time in
Hampstead with Mrs Desmoulins, a young widow from
Lichfield, who sometimes allowed him to console himself
by fondling her. No wonder his next poem, *The Vanity
of Human Wishes,* was pervaded by a dark, distressing
melancholy that his stoic Christian fortitude could not
disguise.

Yet Johnson was still determined to overcome his
difficulties and he still had friends. Garrick, now the rage
of London and the successful manager of Drury Lane,

staged *Irene* with himself as Demetrius and Spranger
Barry as Mahomet. No expense was spared on the scenery
and the costumes, and Johnson for once, expecting to
equal the success Addison had achieved with *Cato*, dis-
carded his dirty linen and his old snuff-coloured coat to
appear at the first performance in a scarlet waistcoat
trimmed with gold lace and a gold-laced hat. Unhappily
his gaudy attire did not influence the public in favour of
his tragedy, which belonged to an outmoded classical
form. It was not enhanced either by the murder of the
heroine being acted on the stage with too much realism by
Mrs Pritchard to a chorus of cat-calls from the auditorium
as the bowstring tightened round her neck. One member
of the audience, however, an attractive, ambitious young
musician named Charles Burney, was excited and fascinated. Like Johnson he was fighting his way up from a
humble provincial background and educating himself as
he went along. First at Shrewsbury, then at Chester, he
had shown a remarkable talent for music, and at the age of
eighteen had eagerly accepted an offer to become the
pupil-apprentice of Dr Arne. That this could mean 'total
dependence on a master', who might turn out to be
'avaricious, selfish, sordid and tyrannical' never occurred
to him at the time—it was a glorious opportunity of
coming to London; and although Dr Arne proved to be
all these things and more, deliberately exploiting the
talents of his pupil for his own gain. Burney was thrilled
to find himself among the best singers and musicians in the
capital, besides discovering that his own charm and
intelligence commended him to one of the most sophisticated and fashionable music-lovers of the nobility, Fulke
Greville.

They were introduced by Kirkman, the famous
harpsichord-maker, Greville having challenged Kirkman
to find him a musician, who had 'a mind and cultivation as
well as finger and ear', talents which the enthusiastic

young Burney already showed and which the thirty-year-old aristocrat was quick to perceive. The attraction was mutual. Greville had everything Burney admired most—breeding, intelligence and wealth; and he had made the most of his opportunities, travelling extensively on the Continent with two French horn players in attendance and studying the music of France and Italy with great sensibility. At home he entertained large parties of persons of high rank and fashion at his splendid country house in Wiltshire, combining his pleasure in the arts with a passion for riding, hunting, playing tennis and gambling, and being able to indulge in whatever diversion he chose to enjoy. He spent the season in town and part of the summer at Bath, where he took Burney on a visit which opened the young man's eyes to a wider kind of life than he had yet imagined; and early in 1748, with Burney's help, he eloped with a charming and accomplished young woman, Fanny Macartney.

Burney was still officially apprenticed to his unpleasant master Thomas Arne, but Greville put down £300 to buy him out and the young musician became a member of the household at Wilbury. Fanny Greville was immensely kind to him. Though 'only a musician' he was never sent to 'the second table' and she tactfully called him 'the youth, to steer clear of the too high title of young gentleman or the too degrading address of boy or young man'. Likewise 'her counsel, conversation and love of literature rendered his abode in the family at once delightful and useful to him during the rest of his life'. He learnt to mix in high society and to enjoy their patronage without losing his own individuality or his pride in being a professional musician, just as Garrick, an actor with the manners of a gentleman, was teaching the nobility to revalue their attitude towards the theatrical profession. Both, indeed, were innovators in developing a more flexible and subtle relationship between the upper classes and the people they employed to amuse them in their hours of leisure; both by their own abilities had raised themselves up from a modest middle-class background to make their mark in the world of the privileged aristocracy.

None the less, by the time Burney had conceived his great admiration for Samuel Johnson, his circumstances had changed. He had fallen in love with Esther Sleepe, 'a young person of beauty, wit, captivating manners and prudent conduct'—though perhaps not quite so prudent as suggested, since their very hasty marriage took place a month after the birth of their first child. Greville rather reluctantly released his protégé and Burney returned to London where he quickly made a reputation as a solo player on the harpsichord, as a fashionable music-teacher and as a composer of incidental pieces for Drury Lane. Then, suddenly, a mysterious fever attacked him, 'with a low consumptive cough and night sweats' and his tender state of health forced him to leave London for King's Lynn in Norfolk, where he was offered the post of organist at St Margaret's Church. He was devastated. 'The bad Organ and the Ignorance of my Auditors must totally extinguish the few Sparks of Genius for Composition I may have and entirely Discourage Practice,' he wrote, 'for Wherein wou'd any pains I took to Execute a Meritorious tho' Difficult Piece of Music be repaid if like Orpheus I am to perform to Stocks and Trees?' Poor Burney, his first sight of the town and of the Norfolk squires mad on horses, pigs and turnips, drove him to despair.

Yet there were compensations. Provincial society was becoming more sophisticated. King's Lynn was not such a cultural desert as he had imagined. The more interesting inhabitants of the town and the surrounding country vied with each other in entertaining so distinguished a musician from the metropolis and soon he was invited everywhere, being held in the highest esteem for his powers of conversation and his agreeable manners no less than for his performance on the harpsichord. Horace Walpole's eccentric nephew, the third Earl of Orford, received him at Houghton and another visitor there, 'a man of strong parts with much wit and Italian humour', Vincenzo Martinelli, encouraged him to study Italian. In fact he taught himself to read the Italian poets while riding on horseback along the Norfolk roads from one music lesson to another, for he was eager to improve his knowledge and never for a moment idle. Success with the ladies who studied the harpsichord with him, had no ill effect on his charming nature. Still being somewhat sensitive about his status among them, he was grateful to Mrs Mackenzie of Narborough for not treating him as 'a mere musician' and delighted when Mrs Stephen Allen, the most elegant lady in Lynn, mistook him for a young undergraduate from Cambridge. Out and about in their society, he continually pursued the pleasure of satisfying his ardent intellectual curiosity and at home with his wife and children, he undertook a course of reading, which covered 'history, voyages, poetry and science' and absolutely everything that came from the pen of Samuel Johnson.

Johnson had started writing a series of essays called the *Rambler* in 1750 and continued through the next ten years with the *Adventurer* and the *Idler*. He had the same purpose as Addison and Steele earlier in the century—to mix morality with wit and to extol the virtue of good behaviour. Though his style was heavier than his predecessors', the mood of the middle of the century was more sober and more given to moralizing than the decade which had produced the *Spectator*, and as a result the essays had a powerful influence on the public as well as satisfying their need for guidance in the moral precepts they now considered necessary to a good life. Burney believed every word of the *Rambler* and the *Idler* and was equally enthusiastic about Johnson's *Dictionary*, which at last appeared in 1755 after nearly nine years' labour and at once established him as the leading scholar of his generation.

For a man whose temperament inclined him towards idleness and ease, it was a stupendous achievement. The hack-writer had become the Great Lexicographer, 'without one act of assistance, one word of encouragement or one smile of favour' from his haughty and neglectful patron; the shabby and eccentric youth from the provinces, a dominating personality in the intellectual life of the metropolis. He was now a widower and, before he accepted a pension of £300 a year from King George III, still very poor. But Oxford honoured him with a degree and when he moved to chambers in the Inner Temple Lane, he lived 'in total idleness and the pride of literature' with Miss Williams, a blind lady who presided over his tea-table, and a faithful Negro servant, Francis Barber. He went abroad at four o'clock in the afternoon, a huge shambling figure in a baggy coat and with a bushy wig singed in front by the candle-flame he was in the habit of reading by, and did not return home until two or three o'clock in the morning, always ending up in one of his favourite taverns in and around Fleet Street, not to drink anything much except lemonade, but to meet his friends; for like Mr Sober in the *Idler*, his chief pleasure was conversation and 'he trembled at the thought of going home alone to the silence of his own chamber'.

New friends gathered round him: men of a similar provincial background making their way upwards—with or without the help of aristocratic patronage—to create a new intellectual force in the world of art and letters. Joshua Reynolds was the son of a scholarly but inefficient Devonshire schoolmaster, who dabbled in astrology, medicine and pharmacology. After three or four years in London apprenticed to the fashionable portrait-painter Thomas Hudson, who introduced him to the convivial gatherings of artists at Old Slaughter's Coffee House in St Martin's Lane, he travelled to Italy as a guest of Captain Keppel and studied in Rome. He did not think much of the rich, empty-headed young Englishmen he met there, travelling about on the Grand Tour with their extravagant retinue of servants, their horses and dogs and their Italian mistresses, their haughty manners and their elaborate velvet coats trimmed with fur. 'There are some men of culture who seek for knowledge,' he wrote, 'but they are few in number. Most of them have a hired carriage stationed in the Piazza di Spagna, which waits for them throughout the day, while they get through it by playing billiards or some other game with each other.' He was not beguiled by the temptations of a foreign city, either. He lived frugally, determined 'to seek for knowledge', studying and copying the works of Raphael and Michelangelo with the utmost diligence and going on to Venice to absorb into his own style the mastery of tone and the glowing colour of Titian, Tintoretto and Veronese.

Returning to England in 1752, he spent a few months in Devonshire before coming to London with his sister Fanny and taking lodgings in St Martin's Lane. Within a year he had moved to a larger studio in Great Newport Street and had become the most successful and the most fashionable portrait-painter in town. Great noblemen and their ladies arrived in their elegant carriages outside his door, stepped over the muddy cobblestones and mounted the stairs to his studio to pose in various classical attitudes flattering to their self-esteem and highly decorative when framed and hung upon the walls of their opulent mansions. Famous beauties of the demi-monde with not very respectable origins, but great fascination—Nelly O'Brien, the mistress of Lord Bolingbroke, and Kitty Fischer, a courtesan with ravishing blue eyes and raven-black hair—sat to him often for the sheer pleasure he took in painting them. Adorable, curly-headed children of the wealthy upper classes frolicked on the studio floor in frilly dresses, with their pet dogs and their toys, to be immortalized for ever in the freshness of their youth; and sometimes a footman was sent round by a rich Milord with a dog on a leash to be painted on its own.

On all occasions Reynolds convinced his noble patrons that he was a master of the Grand Style they had previously admired so much on their travels abroad—as indeed, he was, having applied the discoveries of the Old Masters to the stereotyped art of 'face painting' in a way that none of his English predecessors had ever attempted. Very soon he was having to employ a number of assistants to paint the draperies, the landscapes and the effects he introduced into his compositions, though he worked from nine o'clock in the morning until the light failed him and still found time for diversion in the evenings, either at playing cards or drinking—very moderately—at Old Slaughter's Coffee House. In 1756 he met Johnson for the first time at a party given by the Misses Cotterell, and in spite of the fact that Johnson knew nothing about painting, Reynolds was immediately drawn towards him, inviting him back to Great Newport Street for supper. It was the beginning of a lifelong friendship between them which matured steadily through the years and saw the founding of the Literary Club in 1763 and of the Royal Academy in 1768. 'Johnson may have been said to have formed my mind and to have brushed off from it a load of rubbish,' Reynolds wrote years later; and for Johnson, Reynolds was 'a man not to be spoiled by prosperity'. They remained devoted to each other, however tiresome Johnson's habit of arriving unannounced at Miss Fanny's tea-table might become, or however querulous and tyrannical Reynolds might be to his sister when Johnson at last left them to go home. Reynolds was ambitious to become a scholar as well as a successful artist and to enhance the status of the arts by his own erudition; from Johnson he learnt to follow the logic of an argument and to thrash out his own ideas, sitting for hours on end with his ear-trumpet tuned to the deliberate speech of the greatest talker in London.

The Club—by no means the first or the last to be associated with Johnson—met at the Turk's Head in Gerrard Street not far from Reynold's new house in Leicester Fields. Edmund Burke, who in Johnson's estimation was 'a great man by nature' and one of the most brilliant talkers he had ever met, was a member. 'Take up whatever topic you please, he is ready to meet you,' Johnson declared, and on another occasion: 'That fellow calls forth all my powers.' Young and fiery and very Irish, Burke was sometimes too fond of the bottle but, like Reynolds, a friend for life. So was Bennet Langton, a tall, slender young man resembling a stork standing on one leg, who was a great favourite with the ladies, especially when he attended Mrs Montagu's breakfast parties in Hill Street. He came of an old Lincolnshire family, was a fine scholar with 'a sprightly wit' and so impressed by Johnson's conversation he could never have enough of it. Neither could his fellow undergraduate, Topham Beauclerk, a descendant on the wrong side of the blanket of Charles II with something of the Restoration rake in his character and a great deal of charm. The pair of them once called at Johnson's lodgings by surprise at three o'clock in the morning and took him for 'a frisk' through Covent Garden, ending up by rowing a boat to Billingsgate. Their youth and gaiety gave Johnson tremendous pleasure and helped him to forget that he was growing old. He loved them both—and he loved Oliver Goldsmith, a feckless Irish genius, who had suffered the same kind of failure as himself through an unhappy childhood of poverty and frustration.

Goldsmith had reached London in 1756 at the age of twenty-eight, after two years' travelling on foot on the

Continent, playing the flute and singing for his supper as he begged his way through the towns and villages of France and Switzerland. Like Johnson, he was indolent by nature and uncouth in appearance, though more of a vagabond at heart and totally incapable of improving his circumstances. He had tried the church, law, medicine and schoolmastering all to no effect, since he was far happier loafing around among people even poorer than himself than trying to live a settled existence. Any money he got from friends or relations, he squandered immediately, and the only time he was ever in funds was while he lodged with Mrs Elizabeth Fleming in Islington. This lady received direct from Newbery, the bookseller, all the monies advanced to him for his hack work and kept a meticulous account of everything she bought for him: a bottle of port at 2s, wine and cakes at 1s 6d, eight pens at 2¼d, ten sheets of paper at 5d and a quantity of Sassafras from the chemist's at 6d. She charged £12 10s for three months' board and 18s 0½d for his washing, and entered into her statement £0 0s 0d for the dinners she had generously given to him and some of his friends for nothing.

Such financial security did not, however, last for long or cure Goldsmith of his hopeless improvidence. He had a great fancy for fine clothing and ran up a tailor's bill for a red velvet suit he could never hope to pay for and was equally quixotic with the money he borrowed to settle some of his other debts, giving it away to some of his destitute neighbours instead. One cold night he was found sleeping in the ticking of his bed because he had given the bed-clothes away to a poor woman, and on another occasion when Johnson rescued him from the sheriff's officer with a guinea, he promptly sent out for a bottle of madeira and was only brought to his senses by Johnson putting the cork firmly into the bottle and begging him to remain calm, while he went off with a

dog-eared draft of *The Vicar of Wakefield* to raise money
on it from a bookseller. The money did not go very far,
but the quality of the writing and the fame of the book
greatly enhanced Goldsmith's reputation among his
friends. He was very apt to show off in company and to
suffer from a nervous confusion of thought, which often
made him say or do foolish things, though everyone
always forgave him and loved him for his frailties—
everyone except Boswell, who was jealous of his intimacy
with Johnson.

Boswell came to London in 1762 intent on getting a
commission in the Foot Guards. He wanted to appear as a
brilliant, high-born man of pleasure, poised, sophisticated
and ever in command of himself; in fact, he was a raw,
insecure boy of twenty-two, at odds with his upright and
obstinate father, the Laird of Auchinleck, uncertain of his
own proper direction and much given to fornication,
which he enjoyed briefly but regretted later. Moodiness,
depression and lack of self-confidence constantly interfered
with his high animal spirits and his greed for excitement.
When he saw London from the top of Highgate Hill, he
gave 'three huzzas' and burst into a bawdy song he had
just made up about a pretty girl; he was 'all life and joy'
and his soul 'bounded forth to a certain prospect of happy
futurity'. Less than a week later, after a bad dream and
wondering how he was going to manage on his meagre
allowance of £200 a year, he 'lay abed very gloomy',
thinking that London was doing him no good and that he
might have to go back to Edinburgh with his tail between
his legs.

An invitation to dine with Lord Eglinton made him
feel much better. They went in a coach to Covent Garden
Theatre and upstairs to a handsome room where the
Beefsteak Club met, with Lord Sandwich—'a jolly, hearty,
lively man'—in the chair and Mr Beard, the famous singer
and manager of the Theatre among the company. Lord

Eglinton was a bachelor, good at dancing and fencing and amusing himself around the town. He kept a mistress called Mrs Brown, a quiet, good-humoured lady, 'diligent at slight pretty work and with a degree of laughing simplicity that sometimes appeared foolish'; but he was a man of 'uncommon genius for everything: strong good sense, great quickness of apprehension and liveliness of fancy' and well worth cultivating, since he was a friend of Lord Bute the Prime Minister and a Lord of the Bed-chamber. Boswell had larked around with him on a previous visit to London and he flattered himself that Lord Eglinton found his company very agreeable, especially after he had bought 'a genteel, violet-coloured frock suit' to wear when they went abroad together.

None the less there were terrible ups and downs of splendour and misery in young Boswell's reactions to the delights of the metropolis. His chances of getting a commission dwindled week by week and it was a wry compensation to be able to watch the Guards drilling in St James's Park. More fun was to be had there after sunset when the ladies of the Court in their bright satins and dainty shoes retired and the ladies of the town sauntered in among the bushes and down the long avenue by the canal. One of them was a young Shropshire girl, only seventeen and 'very well-looked', to be had for 6d; another called Nanny Baker was 'a strong, plump, good-humoured girl' he picked up on his way through the Park to Drury Lane Theatre. But sometimes when he felt the urge upon him, the girls were ugly, dirty and nameless and Boswell hustled them into a back-court or alley-way off Fleet Street on his way home from a tavern, vowing when he got back to his lodgings in Downing Street that he would never be so foolish again. A more extended affair with a handsome actress, involving him in a voluptuous night at the Black Lion in Water Lane, where they arrived in a hackney-coach 'like any decent couple' with their night-clothes in a bag and some almond biscuits, led him into serious trouble, and pride in his 'god-like vigour at the game' ended in expensive doctors' bills and six weeks' total abstinence from sexual indulgence.

He did his best to talk himself into believing that pleasure was not entirely dependent on Venus and made a virtuous attempt to reform his way of life by studying philosophy and history; but the world was waiting on his doorstep to be explored and as soon as his symptoms eased off a little, he went out and about again with his young friend the Hon Andrew Erskine and his sister Lady Betty Macfarlane, who had married 'a greasy, rotten old carcass' for his money and kept open house in Leicester Street. Higher up the social scale and much more desirable in consequence were the ostentatious routs at Northumberland House given by the Countess and her husband, who had inherited the pride and the enormous wealth of the Percy family. Not knowing anyone there and the richly adorned rooms being 'full of the best company', Boswell felt a little anxious until Lady Northumberland singled him out 'with the greatest complacency and kindness, being easy and affable' and he thought people were looking at him with envy 'as a man of some distinction and a favourite of my Lady's'. He hoped she would use her influence to help him get his commission in the Guards and was bitterly disillusioned when she failed him. 'O these Great People! They are a sad set of beings,' he wrote. 'This woman who seemed so cordially my friend and promised me her good offices so strongly is, I fear, a fallacious hussy.'

He had better luck with his less high-ranking friends. Thomas Sheridan, the Irish actor, and his clever wife constantly invited him to their house and though Sheridan was a difficult, self-opinionated man, quick to take offence and very unforgiving, Mrs Sheridan was hospitable and very sensible. Garrick was even more amiable.

Boswell's fulsome praise of his acting flattered his vanity
and he invited him to 'a genteel breakfast' in Southampton Street. They walked together in his library, 'a
handsome room with a pretty large collection of good
books and some busts and pictures', Boswell looking
forward to 'the pleasing prospect' of the many happy
hours he would enjoy there in the future among all the
men of genius of the age. Garrick told him that he would
be a very great man, which sent him into raptures of
delight, 'for really, to speak seriously', he wrote, 'I think
there is a blossom about me of something more distinguished than the generality of mankind.' He then
indulged in 'noble reveries of having a regiment and
getting into Parliament, of making a figure and becoming
a man of consequence in the state'—the kind of wishful
thinking that occupied so much of his leisure and was
faithfully recorded day after day in his Journal. What he
did not know was that his talent for reporting every
detail of his own life would one day make him a figure of
quite extraordinary consequence; nor did he realize that
destiny was waiting for him on the afternoon of 16 May
1763, when he drank tea with Mr Davies in his bookshop
in Russell Street and the great Mr Samuel Johnson, 'whom
he had so long wished to see', walked in.

Johnson knocked him down; and Boswell's first
impression was of 'a man of a most dreadful appearance—
a very big man, troubled with sore eyes, the palsy and the
King's evil, slovenly in his dress and with a most uncouth
voice'. He rapped out at Boswell for being a Scot and
snubbed him when he dared to speak of Garrick. Yet a
week later, after a hilarious night with two women one
after the other at the Shakespeare Head Tavern, Boswell
went to call on him in the Inner Temple. The scholar's
pleasure at being visited in his untidy cell was even
greater than the neophyte's in visiting the high priest of
literature. Johnson begged him to stay, glad of his

company—of any company that mitigated his fear of being left alone. Here was a new audience, a brash, eager young man with a soft centre, an infinite capacity for listening and answering back with the right kind of provocative deference; a young man who needed a hero to worship and guidance in solving his problems.

Before long Boswell was entertaining his new acquaintance at the Mitre Tavern in Fleet Street and writing: 'He was much pleased with my ingenuous open way and he cried: "Give me your hand. I have taken a liking to you."' They sat up until two o'clock in the morning with a couple of bottles of port between them and Boswell went home in high exultation, having told him 'all my story'. A week or so later at another supper party, which included Goldsmith and Davies as well as Johnson, 'well dressed and in excellent spirits, neither muddy nor flashy', Boswell sat 'with much secret pride. thinking of my having such a company with me . . . and gently assisting the conversation by those little arts which serve to make people throw out their sentiments with ease and freedom.' Again he went home in a state of the utmost satisfaction, pleased with himself and his liberality, having had 'more enjoyment of my money this evening than if I had spent it in one of your splendid Court-end taverns among a parcel of people that I did not care a farthing for . . . and having received this night both instruction and pleasure.'

But his time in London was running out, his father having agreed to send him abroad to study law after his failure to get a commission. Johnson assured him that he was lucky to escape going into the Guards, as he was 'already past those puerilities'; and with this consolation and still more evidence of the great man's affection for him, Boswell had to be content. They had a marvellous trip down to Greenwich one day by water, being 'entertained with the immense number and variety of ships

lying at anchor . . . and charmed with the beautiful fields
on each side of the river'. Johnson talked about the
Methodists and of the great success they were having with
the common people by preaching to them in a way they
could understand and his own sympathy with the predica-
ment of the poor impressed Boswell deeply. They then
got back to the subject of Boswell's future, a topic that
never ceased to absorb him, and Johnson promised to go
down to Harwich with him to see him off on his travels
four days later. When he did so, he was immensely helpful,
'rousing him with manly and spirited conversation', and
they embraced and parted with tenderness on the beach.
Boswell went on board and watched him for a considerable
time 'while he remained rolling his majestic frame in the
usual manner', until at last he turned away towards the
town and disappeared.

Boswell stayed in Europe for two and a half years,
flirting with the ladies of polite society in Holland,
Germany and Italy, picking up girls in the street and
pursuing the great men of the century—Rousseau, Voltaire
and General Paoli, the heroic leader of the Corsican revolt
against the Genoese invaders. He was sometimes gay and
sometimes very miserable in his efforts to combine education with pleasure and to show himself off to the best
advantage. He considered marrying the beautiful Zélide,
a savante and *bel esprit* of the Dutch aristocracy, but she
would not have him. He put on a Scots bonnet at the
King's parade in Potsdam, hoping to draw the attention
of Frederick the Great to his person, but the King did
not look at him; 'However,' he wrote, 'I was pleased to
have shewn the first blue bonnet on the Prussian Parade.'
At Môtiers, near Neuchâtel, he managed to gain access
to Rousseau by flattering his housekeeper and mistress,
Thérèse Le Vasseur; and at Ferney, he obtained an invitation to stay the night with Voltaire, ingratiating himself
with this most celebrated man of letters in all Europe by

the boldness of his attack. In Naples he met the notorious Wilkes, exiled from England after his onslaught on the establishment, and rioted around with him, playing the role of Don Juan with a tragi-comic affectation of manliness and dissipation. Then he joined Lord Mountstuart, the son of Lord Bute, a handsome, convivial young man with 'elegant manners and a tempestuously noble soul', but fell out with him and went off on his own to Corsica. It was a daring adventure, which entailed much hard travelling on foot through wild, mountainous country to Corte and another ninety miles on to Sollacarò, where he at last caught up with Paoli and was received with a civility that flattered his self-esteem and increased his admiration for the Corsican hero.

Johnson, meanwhile, though lazy about writing letters, did not forget his young friend, and his own life was moving into a new phase of ease and splendour. In 1765 Arthur Murphy, the Irish actor, introduced him to Henry Thrale and his wife Hester, and they became his dearest friends. Thrale was a prosperous, well-educated brewer belonging to the new class of rich merchants who had made their mark in society, a Member of Parliament and a liberal host. He had a town house near his brewery in Southwark and an elegant villa six miles out in the village of Streatham. Hester was still in her early twenties, a small, vivacious young woman, whose ambition to become the mistress of a salon that would surpass Mrs Montagu's was heightened by Johnson's immediate response to her feminine sympathy. Mrs Montagu sought friendship and equality with the opposite sex through her own capacity for learned discussion. Her parties at Hill Street were formal and ceremonious; everyone sat around in a stiff circle and paid court to her as the Queen of the Blue Stockings. Johnson admired 'her constant stream of conversation, her learning without pedantry, her judgement and her politeness', and he admired her bosom

friends Mrs Carter, Mrs Boscawen and Mrs Vesey. They
were all very erudite; Hester was not—but she had
enthusiasm, gaiety and the desire to please and she took
possession of Johnson's heart.

She offered him comfort and affection. A room was set
aside for him at Streatham, the library restocked with
books and a summer-house built in the garden for his
use. Everything that could be done for his pleasure was
done; for besides being proud of her possession of the
most celebrated lion of the age, whose intellectual friends
added lustre to her drawing-room when they came to visit
him, Hester was genuinely fond of him, surrounding him
with ease and softness and a luxury he had never known
before. His favourite dishes—a leg of pork boiled until it
dropped from the bone or a veal pie with plums and
sugar—were put in front of him and nothing was said if
he took a second helping of lobster sauce with his plum
pudding or gobbled up a dish of stewed carp with the aid
of his fingers. He could consume seven or eight large
peaches out of the garden before breakfast and souse his
coffee in cream or melted butter, while his prodigious
appetite for tea drinking and sitting up late at night was
freely indulged, even when Hester was dropping with
exhaustion. She did not mind—or not in the beginning; he
gave her something her husband and her children had not
been able to satisfy—a sense of her own importance and of
being needed. And she had captured him, had almost
tamed him—this giant, whose conversation could explode
and kill, yet of whom she wrote: 'He gave away all he
had. All he did was gentle, if all he said was rough.'
Some years hence when he was old and awkward and her
heart was touched by a younger man, they would hurt
each other most cruelly, but not yet. For the moment it
was enough for Johnson to write when he was away from
Streatham: 'I long to come to that place which my dear
friends allow me to call *home*.'

7

COUNTRY DIVERSIONS

DR JOHNSON DECLARED that it was 'very strange and very melancholy, that the paucity of human pleasures should persuade us ever to call hunting one of them'; he thought it was 'no diversion at all and never took a man out of himself for a moment'. But he was wrong. Sport was an instinctive passion with the English aristocracy and their love of hunting a more important contribution to the general welfare of the nation than Johnson had the wit to realize. For unlike the French *noblesse*, the English land-owners with their splendid houses, their glorious gardens and their highly developed taste in the arts, were as easy in the stables with their grooms and huntsmen as in their state apartments when giving a ball or a banquet, and their affection for their horses and their dogs was shared by the country folk who depended on them for whatever work or enjoyment was to be had on their vast estates. Indoors the aristocratic world of power and affluence might be exclusive; but out of doors the duke or the lord of the manor was on nodding terms with everyone in the village and his heart was in the land he owned.

Sir Robert Walpole, born and bred at Houghton, found more relaxation in hunting whenever he returned to Norfolk than in anything else. It demanded good horsemanship and skill in outwitting the fox or the hare, and for a man who had spent his whole life outwitting his political opponents, it was a refreshing change from the complicated intrigues of the Court. The bright air of the country also gave him a huge appetite. After a day's hunting with his guests, he sat them down to a dinner 'up to the chin in beef, venison, geese, turkeys, etc. and generally over the chin in claret, strong beer and punch'. He was never ashamed of showing off the immense wealth he had acquired by somewhat devious means, and his hospitality was lavish in the extreme as befitted the Chief Minister of the Crown. In 1733 he spent £1,118 12s 6d with his wine-merchant, James Bennett, and in spite of buying much of his claret and his burgundy in hogsheads, returned 552 dozen empty bottles to him at the end of the year.

Out of office at last after twenty-two years in the service of King George II and Queen Caroline, Sir Robert retired to Norfolk as Earl of Orford and grew lyrical about the countryside. 'Men of Witt and Pleasure about Town, understand not the Language, nor Taste the Charms of the Inanimate World,' he wrote to a friend. 'My Flatterers are all Mutes, the Oakes, the Beeches, the Chestnutts seem to Contend which shall best please the Lord of the Manor. They cannot deceive, they will not Lye, I in return, with Sincerity, admire them and have as many Beauties about me as fill up all my hours of Dangling.' But he only lived a year or two longer to enjoy his leisure and the felicity of coming home to the great house he had rebuilt and furnished with such extravagant taste, sending to Italy for the choicest Genoa velvets, tapestries, chimney-pieces and paintings that money could buy. Perhaps when he strolled through his picture-gallery, he remembered that his pocket-money as a boy had amounted to 2s a year and that his hats and neckerchieves had been bought cheaply at Lynn Fair by his prudent mother. Perhaps he remembered hunting the fields in his youth, for his enthusiasm for his native county was genuine and his love of sport had never been diluted by the affectations of the Court and society. It was said that a letter from his huntsman or his gamekeeper always took precedence over any political dispatch he received when he was in office, and he was just as happy—sometimes happier—swopping coarse stories with his country neighbours as in the Queen's drawing-room, measuring every word he said. He did not share the views of Lord Chesterfield, who wrote in one of his admonitory letters to his illegitimate son: 'Eat as much game as you please, but I hope you will never kill any yourself; and indeed, I think you are above any of these rustic, illiberal Sports of guns, dogs and horses which characterize our English Bumpkin Country Gentlemen.'

It was the fashionable thing for the sophisticated townsman with his perfume and his pomade to despise the country gentleman stinking of the stables and the fields. Ever since the Restoration, the squire with his brutal manners, randy horseplay and voracious appetite for life, had been represented as a comic absurdity in the theatre. His visits to London with his wife and daughters aping the fashions of the town, were mocked unmercifully and his crude behaviour set in the most unseemly light. Yet there were many men of good education besides the great patrician landlords, who loved the country and hated the town and whose love of sport yielded them immense satisfaction. Sir Thomas Cave of Stanford Park in Leicestershire, wrote of his longing for 'the wholesom countrey air ... being almost suffocated with the nauseousness of London'. Not from choice, but as a Member of Parliament seriously concerned with doing his duty, he was forced to spend some time every year at Westminster, with or without his charming wife, Margaret, who shared his interests in the country and disliked the fatigue of town life as much as he did. Margaret was the daughter of Sir John Verney, later Viscount Fermanagh of Claydon, Buckinghamshire, and the two families, brought up to enjoy life in the country, kept in close touch with each other through constant journeys, often fraught with danger and anxiety, between Claydon and Stanford, and through the long letters they never failed to write when visiting was impossible.

Sir Thomas was a devoted husband. 'When women is taken in the Plurall number, I don't love 'em much,' he wrote to his father-in-law, 'for the Singular number is Sufficient for me and then I love it dearly'; and the reception Margaret met with as a bride when she first went to Stanford was highly gratifying. 'The Country has been extremely civil and shows abundance of Rejoycing and respect at our comeing, severall times comeing to meet us with wonderful Treats of Sweetmeats and Cool Tankards by the Way and the bells ringing at every town we came thro',' she wrote, and besides this the servants took a great liking to their new mistress and did everything in their power to make her happy and comfortable. Stanford Hall was an unpretentious stone house with a charming outlook. The park was well timbered and green with fallow deer browsing in the cool shade of the trees and swans moving placidly on the lake, and Leicestershire was wonderful hunting country. 'My very pretty busy beagles are, I tell you, the best in Great Brittain,' Sir Thomas wrote to his young brother-in-law Ralph Verney, and he often sent his hounds and his horses ahead of him when he went on a visit to Claydon. Kept in London in January by political business, he wrote longingly: 'The weather being so seasonable, I hope you had good Sport a hunting. It being a harty wish from me since your Delight

I

is chiefly in that particular Diversion'; then he asked Ralph 'to bidd Jack take my Bay Horse out with you once per week, if well enough, to keep him in breath against my coming down'.

Sir Thomas bred some of his own horses at Stanford and was as proud of them as of his beagles. 'The Grey Mare is sound, I may say there's not the fellow of her for pleasure, except it be a sister of her wich I have now bred, 5 years old, gallops fine and trots easy and well,' he told Ralph; and he urged his brother-in-law to come over to Stanford Hall for the races at Quainton, where another of his favourite horses would be running against stiff opposition from those of the neighbouring squires. This kind of amateur riding and racing when three or four of the local gentry got together for their own amusement, went on all over the country outside the regular race-meetings at Newmarket, Epsom or Doncaster, and Sir Thomas was a keen supporter of every contest within reach of his own home. At Loughborough his horse was fairly beaten and the cup won by 'an honest Northampton-shire innkeeper', but at Lutterworth he was more success-ful. On this occasion, returning from London, he found that his wife, who had been ill and was living on asses' milk, had entered one of his horses for the race and he wrote off at once to his father-in-law: 'By Virtue of his fleet heales, he wonn the Tankard, which is a very good one to drink Asses Milk out of, it being somewhat large.' After the race was over 'the Ladyes went to Mrs Coles's and there spent the night in Dancing and Cards and other Neighbourly Divertions till one of the clock in the morning'.

Lady Cave's health was somewhat precarious and she often had to resort to asses' milk or to the still worse remedies of cupping, bleeding, purging and sweating recommended by the doctors of the eighteenth century. But she enjoyed rural life, even in the winter when

communication between one household and another was
often impossible. Having had a household of guests
staying all through the autumn, she wrote to her father:
'They have now agreed to leave us alone, to the comfort and enjoyment of Long Evenings and Dark Dayes,
which Sir Thomas and his Sports will pass off and be
pleased with so long a Playtime.' By Christmas she
was sending her father a 'fatt Swan' and recommending
him to try it 'in a Pye'. With three young children
and another due at any moment, the Caves were unable
to get to Claydon for the festive season, so the swan,
which was a rarity in Buckinghamshire, was consumed
by Lord Fermanagh and some of his near neighbours,
Squire Abel of East Claydon, the Reverend William
Butterfield, rector of Middle Claydon, with their wives
and families.

The duty of entertaining all the farmers, villagers and
ragtag and bobtail of the neighbourhood fell rather
heavily on Lord Fermanagh as Lord of the Manor and
Knight of the Shire. It was the custom for the waits and
the wassailers, the hand-bell ringers and the mummers to
arrive at all hours of the day or night and for them to be
feasted on beef and plum pudding. The fun went on for
days; the mummers acted their Christmas play of St
George and the Dragon, with Beelzebub and the Prince
of Paradine as major characters, in the big barns of the
home-farm, and the wassail bowl was filled again and again
with spiced ale and gifts of money. 'Our house is every
day full of country people, like an Election time,' Lord
Fermanagh wrote. 'It has been a troublesome time. Every
day with the noise of Either Drums, Trumpets, Hautboys, Pipes or Fiddles, some days 400 Guests, very few
under a 100, that besides the vast expense it has been very
tiresome.' After it was all over 'a Fitt of the Gout tooke
him in the Foot' and he wisely retired to the peace of his
own chamber to be cosseted by Lady Fermanagh, who

adored him and addressed him in her letters as 'My Jewell' or 'My Deare Heart'.

Lady Fermanagh was an excellent housewife. She coped brilliantly with all her husband's affairs at Claydon during his frequent absences in London for the parliamentary sessions and was never idle. If she was not making wines from 'Civill oringes' or primrose water to help his gout, she was chasing the gardener round, showing him where to plant a new 'Nectrin tree' against the south wall in the gooseberry garden, or ticking the servants off for drinking up all the 'small beere' and unpacking the barrels of oysters which Lord Fermanagh sent down from London by John Innes, the carrier, sniffing them very carefully if they looked at all off colour. Fish was always a problem. Five ponds in the park at Claydon were stocked with 'Large Carpes' and there was some trout-fishing on the estate; but soles and smelts, lobsters and fresh salmon had to come by the carrier in the down-box and were not always so fresh as they might be if Innes dallied by the way, while Lady Fermanagh did not always trust him to look after the up-box she sent to her husband stuffed with ducklings, 'a fine Pigg' and more primrose water to keep him going in London. Among the luxuries she commissioned him to buy for her in town were 'Green Tea, the best Coffee, some Aquavitae, Ginger and Loafe Sugar, not having a dust in the house'.

The Whitsun Ales, another country festival of very ancient origin, worried her a good deal, bringing even more disturbances to Claydon than the junketings at Christmas. 'We have such A Bundance of rabble and the worst sort of Company round us that I wish noe mischiefes Happens,' she wrote. 'I can't help giving the Morrises money when they come, for they tell me everybody doing it is the best way to send them going—there is one at Steeple Claydon, one at Hoggshaw, one at Buckingham and one at Stratten Audley, and this minitt the House is full of one of 'em.' There were also a great many 'Substantial freeholders that con't be denyed eating and drinking', which added to the household expenses; besides 'the Rodes being so full of people that fivety will goe by the Mount at a time'. Yet in spite of being somewhat unsympathetic towards the dancing and the merrymaking of the rural folk from round about, Lady Fermanagh was devoted to the country. 'Mrs Dormer's family goes up to town again,' she wrote in the same letter, 'and she wonders att me to stay in the country, and I tell her I wonder att her as much to leave fresh Aire to goe up to the Dusty town.' This retort must have silenced Mrs Dormer very effectively, even if she did not know that Lady Fermanagh had a poor opinion of her husband, Judge Dormer: 'for I thinke him the man that will look one in the face and cut one's throught,' she wrote on another occasion, indicating that she had a mind of her own and was not on the best of terms with the Judge or his lady.

This would have been unfortunate, for the gentry relied on the friendliness of their neighbours when travelling was still perilous, and the diversions of the community as a whole depended to a large extent on the goodwill of the gentry. The noble duke hunting the country with his own pack of hounds was emulated by the squire and the yeomen farmers, the parson and the village schoolmaster. One parson was said to have worn his hunting boots in the pulpit, so that when the morning service was over, he could jump on his horse and join the chase without delay, while everyone else, if they could not borrow or beg a horse, scrambled after the hunt on foot. To see the hare or the fox double back and bolt in the opposite direction and the hounds checked before they sniffed out the scent, was an excitement everyone could understand and talk about endlessly afterwards in the parlour of the local inn through the long, dead winter evenings.

Even when hunting became a more highly organized sport after 1750, when Hugo Meynell, master of the Quorn in Leicestershire, started breeding faster hounds to chase the fox for miles across the country, the spectacle of the huntsmen in their liveries, the hounds in full-cry and the glossy horses galloping after them brought gaiety and colour into the lives of the hard-working country people. But shooting was a different matter. Though the English upper classes were far less autocratic than their continental neighbours, the shooting of game was a privilege they guarded very closely. No one not having an estate worth £40 per annum or goods and chattels worth £200 was allowed by the Game Act to go out with a gun and a dog, or to kill partridges, pheasants, hares and rabbits by snaring or netting; and this inevitably led to poaching, which developed during the century into a disastrous war between the rich and the poor, causing much ill-feeling and much hardship to the unprivileged section of the community.

For the pattern of life in the country was changing. With the increasing enclosure of the land, the small freeholder was being squeezed out by his richer neighbours and the squire of limited means bought up by the wealthy landowners intent upon improving and enlarging their estates. The cottager lost his inalienable right to a strip of common land and was forced to become a wage-earner or to go on the parish if he could no longer support his family. He was given little or no compensation, deprived of his cow, his pig and his own corn and forbidden to kill the plump fowls of the air which might have kept his wife and children from starvation. The sport, in fact, that gave so much pleasure to his master and furnished the high table at the manor with succulent game of all kinds, was really his necessity. He could not be blamed if he took to poaching in his struggle for existence.

Poaching was besides the most exciting drama of rural

life. It needed skill and a steady nerve. It appealed to the
hunting instinct and was part of the perpetual battle
between primitive man and the forces of nature. Because
it was forbidden, it was all the more attractive. It meant
creeping out at night or in the early morning into the
silent woods, fooling the gamekeepers and grabbing
something for nothing with a secret exultation. As time
went on and the severity of the penalties increased, it led
to corruption and gang warfare on a big scale, but in the
middle of the century, farmers, gamekeepers themselves,
otherwise respectable clergymen and even the magistrates
were all involved one way or another in the illicit sport
of poaching. It had an irresistible fascination. 'Some do it
from the love of pursuit of wild creatures, of strolling
about in solitary woods, of night-watching and adventure,' one writer declared, and a very old country labourer
asserted with dignity: 'Us don't see no harm in it, for the
Bible says the wild birds is sent for the poor man as well
as the quality.'

But if the harsh Game Laws divided the rich from the
poor, there were other diversions in the country besides
hunting which brought them together. Cockfighting in
the village churchyard or the ale-house, cock-throwing,
which was even more cruel, bull-baiting and badger-
baiting were enjoyed by all classes until well into the
middle of the century, when the more refined members
of the gentry began to disapprove of the brutality involved in such sports and to leave them to 'the meaner
sort'. Wrestling matches and pugilism attracted the
raffish younger sons of the squirearchy and the nobility
as well as the lads of the village. Sir Thomas Parkyns of
Bunny Park, Nottinghamshire, organized an annual
wrestling meeting on his estate, which drew people from
as far away as Devonshire and Westmorland, though it
took them weeks and months to get there on foot or by
the slow stage-wagons ambling at a snail's pace from one

district to another. Being something of a martinet, Sir Thomas was able to control the behaviour of the crowds to some extent; at other meetings, where huge sums of money were at stake, hooliganism broke out among the punch-drunk spectators and everyone started fighting everyone else in a furious battle of whirling legs and arms. Boxing matches were even worse—for pugilism was a most savage affair, described as 'downright slaughtering' until Jack Broughton, the Champion of England in 1740, brought in a new rule providing the competitors with 'mufflers' or boxing-gloves that would 'effectually secure them from the inconveniency of black eyes, broken jaws and bloody noses'. Not that anyone paid much attention to any of the rules and regulations; Jack Broughton, a protégé of the Duke of Cumberland for ten years, was himself beaten by Jack Slack, who blinded him with a blow between the eyes, and the Duke, having lost several thousand pounds on the match, dropped him like a dead duck.

Tough and ferocious, the professional pugilists had a tremendous following throughout the country and especially at the annual fairs, which took place within reach of almost every country town or village to mark the holy days and the seasons of the year at Easter, Midsummer and Michaelmas. Unlike Bartholomew and Southwark, these local fairs were still of great importance as trading centres, serving a countryside not yet industrialized, besides providing the only holidays in the year for the rural inhabitants in the neighbourhood. There were the sheep fairs in the North and the West Country and the cattle fairs in East Anglia; the horse fairs in the Midlands and the Nottingham Goose Fair; the Mop or Hiring fairs at Stratford on Avon and at Abingdon in Berkshire; the fair at Bury St Edmunds and the great Stourbridge fair, famous since its foundation in the thirteenth century for every kind of merchandise.

Here Defoe saw 'as many coffee houses, taverns, brandy shops and eating houses, all in tents and booths erected overnight in the great cornfield between Cambridge and Newmarket, as in London'. The proclamation of the fair was made by the Grand Marshal, wearing a scarlet coat with purple buttons and leading a splendid procession of civic dignitaries with drums, trumpets and bell-ringers in attendance. Fresh herrings and oysters were sent in from Colchester for the official banquet and there was roast goose, roast pork, gingerbread, gooseberry pie and strong ale for everyone. Trade in wool and hops, wine and cotton, kerseys, fustians, tickings, blankets, and in wrought-iron, brassware, chinaware, hats, haberdashery, toys, pewter and gold, was done by the merchants and manufacturers 'wholly in their pocketbooks' and by word of mouth. Barns and stables in the neighbouring villages were turned into inns to accommodate the huge concourse of people arriving to attend the fair and no one minded the congestion and the stench, the crowds of carts, wagons and coaches all jammed together outside the ground, or the higglers and the butchers, the packhorse-men, the pedlars, minstrels, tumblers, jugglers and mountebanks threading their way in and out of the crush. The confusion was all part of the fun.

Thomas Gray on his tour of the North Country described the people arriving for the great horse fair at Brough Hill in 1769. 'A mile and a half from Brough on a hill lay a great army encamped,' he wrote. 'On nearer approach appeared myriads of horses and cattle on the road itself; and in all the fields round me a brisk stream hurrying across the way; thousands of clean, healthy people in their best parti-coloured apparel, farmers and their families, esquires and their daughters, hastening up from the hills and down the fell on every sides, glittering in the sun and pressing forward to join the throng.' Every road and green track for miles around had strings of ponies and horses travelling along it, and high above the fairground the gipsies were gathered in their wild rags, setting the hill ablaze with bonfires when the fair was over and dancing all night in their garish glow, while the boys and girls from the more domesticated villages round about, gaped in horrid fascination.

These boys and girls at the Mop or Hiring fairs stood in a row with favours in their hats to show their trade, waiting to be hired as servants or labourers and once they had been paid their 'earnest money', were free to go off and enjoy the Punch and Judy shows or to make love in the fields. The milkmaids took the tuft of cowhair out of their caps and tied them up with ribbons bought from a pedlar instead, and the boys, vain of their muscular strength, showed off at shin-kicking or cudgel-throwing, sometimes for prizes which included a gold-laced hat worth a guinea or a pair of buckskin gloves. At Bury St Edmunds they were tempted by a stall-holder from London called Mrs Johnson, who sold 'elecampane, fenugreek, pickles and tumeric', or by a widow aptly named Letitia Rookes, who used her two daughters to entice customers into her booth in the dark of the evening. The yokels had nothing to guide them except their animal instincts, and sometimes they were cunning enough not to be fleeced by the sharpers waiting to pounce on them; but sometimes they drank until they were fuddled and woke up next morning in a ditch with their clothes torn and their pockets empty, wondering what had hit them in the midst of the fun of the fair.

The fairs were the only high days and holidays of their year. They had no leisure from the incessant toil of the seasons and very little pleasure that was not dependent on the life of their own village. They enjoyed gossip, quarrelling with each other, the feuds between parson and squire, the poaching affrays and macabre stories of ghosts and witches told beside the fire to make their hair stand on end. They had little or no aesthetic feeling for the beauty of their surroundings; they took the country for granted and battled with it from dawn until dusk to fill their stomachs with food. Yet subconsciously they belonged to the land and were disorientated when the enclosures forced them to drift away to the towns as casual labourers or to be caught up in the beginnings of the industrial revolution as ill-paid factory workers. The village was their home. They mistrusted 'foreigners'—anyone from outside their own parish—and were generally loyal to the people they knew without losing their stubborn independence and the right of every man to hold his own views if he had any. They respected the gentry and seldom envied them and the gentry in return took their duties towards them seriously. Many a dispute was settled by the squire as Justice of the Peace with dignity and decency and afterwards there was nothing to stop everyone meeting in the ale-house without reproach or at cricket on the village green.

Cricket started as an amusement for the humbler classes with two stumps and a popping-hole between them, a bat curved like an old-fashioned dinner knife and fast bowling along the ground, the score being kept by notches marked on a stick. By 1743, however, it was observed that 'noblemen, gentlemen and clergy were making butchers, cobblers and tinkers their companions in the game', and three years later when Kent scored 111 notches against All England's 110, Lord John Sackville was a member of the winning team and Rumney, the head-gardener at Knole, its captain. Matches were always played for money—and not everyone approved. Ralph Verney wrote: 'There were near 6,000 people at the great Cricket Match yesterday at Wootton. These matches will soon be as pernicious to Poor People as Horse Races, for the contagion spreads.' But pernicious or not, the enthusiasm for cricket gathered pace, spreading from Kent and Hampshire through Sussex, Middlesex and Surrey to the Midlands and the northern counties. New rules were drawn up by the Earl of Winchilsea and the Duke of Richmond, both of them presidents of the Hambledon Cricket Club, and later by Thomas Lord on his first Marylebone Cricket Ground in Dorset Square. The spectators enjoyed themselves as much as the players and while the big matches drew large crowds to admire the skill and the pace of the players, village cricket continued to amuse everyone in the long summer evenings with the squire and the blacksmith, the farmer and the parson all playing amicably together and their wives and children watching the fun.

Farmers' wives worked as hard as their husbands, but if their leisure was scant, their lives were by no means devoid of pleasure. Anne Hughes was married to a prosperous farmer in Herefordshire and having been taught to read and write by her dear Mistress Prue, a daughter of the former squire at the big house, she kept a diary which she wrote up every night when her husband was in bed and asleep. 'I doe much lyke ritinge in mye booke what we doe,' she remarked, 'but I know nott what John woulde saye iff hee didde see itt.' Quite a lot of things she kept from John, not to enrage him or to give him the chance of saying she was extravagant when she helped her poorer neighbours or her pretty little maid, Sarah, on the side; for she understood his ways and knew exactly how to manage him. For one thing she fed him superbly. 'Then I toe thee kitchen toe see all is reddy for John's home cummin, the wile Sarah coms in wyth a fyne goose egge thee first thys yere, wiche I doe putt in thee panne ande cooke for John's tee wyth 2 goode slivvers of ham, and doe putt thee boyled beef ande chese wythe a mete pastie, he bein always verrie emptie when he doe com from market; itt bein a cold daye I doe gett reddy a goode bowle off punche steaming hotte, wiche is as well for hee cumin in verrie crosse wyth thee newes off nott sellen one off the cowes wiche hee doe bring backe.' All this careful preparation worked like a charm; for 'later, beine fedd, he is verrie plesed ande doe saye howe hee didde like thee goose egge, ande what a goode wiffe he hav gott, tow wich,' she added artfully, 'I doe agree seeinge howe I doe putt upp wyth his fandillos ande temper wythoute saying a worde, butt thys I doe nott tell him.'

Sometimes, 'bein a bigge mann ande hartie', John was tempted to over-indulge his appetite: 'When wee doe kille pigges, hee doe lyke thee newe mete soe muche soe doe ett toe his filling, soe making hys innerds paineful.' Then she dosed him firmly with 'thee jouce of a lemmon wyth a pinsh of ginger, ande blacke pepper ande a tayste off salt' after making him swallow some peppercorns first. 'He didde make a mity fusse sayen I shulde kille him wyth mye messes burnin hys innerds,' but she really did know best, for it was 'thee pigges' that died and not the farmer. The boiling and salting of the meat went on for days. Nothing was wasted. The hearts and the tongues were put into jars, the livers fried and the tails chopped up to go in a pie. A nice joint was sent up to Lady Susan, wife of the squire at the big house, the fat was stored, the skinny bits given to the poor and the trotters sent to Parson Ellis's wife, 'knoeing rite well she doe hate them, having no teethe too byte them bein soe froustie'.

Mistress Ellis was not one of Anne's favourite neighbours. 'Shee doe forever rile mee wyth her primms and prissums,' she wrote, 'albeitte a no bodie, her familie bein only poore millers, thoe shee doe sett upp toe bee a ladye'; and Parson Ellis was not popular either, his sermons were 'verrie drye'. Mistress Prue and her sister Livvy were quite another matter; they were 'reele ladies' and unfailingly good to everyone in the village. Besides showing

Anne how to write, Mistress Prue had taught her to play on the spinet, and she was wild with joy when John's mother came on a long visit, 'ridinge packe horse soe too keepe eye on thee waggon toe wiche shee didde carrie divers thinges', including a spinet for her daughter-in-law, which looked 'verrie fyne' in the parlour and was a great success at the party they gave when the pig killings were over, Anne playing 'a merrie jigge wyche didde please all vastlie, John bein verrie proude att mye skille'.

Mother and daughter-in-law got on terribly well together, sometimes ganging up with the little maid Sarah, so that John complained of 'bein plaged wythe petticuts', which made the women laugh uproariously. For they knew what he liked and studied his comforts, making pies and pasties, pickled strawberries and 'Eldern-berrie wine warmed upp wythe a beaten egge and cinnamun'. They scrubbed his house from top to bottom, polishing the warming-pans, the candlesticks and the cooking-pots and making them gleam like moonshine, besides feeding the pigs and the poultry for him, making butter and cheese and helping with the harvest. When they went to church 'cum Sundays', Anne put on her 'black sylk wyth thee wyte spottes' which John had bought for her at the market and her mother-in-law brought out some 'fyne lase' to impress the rest of the congregation, though John was a very unwilling churchgoer and always nodded through Parson Ellis's long-winded sermons.

The two women enjoyed dressing up again when they went to 'drynk tee wyth thee Ladie Susan att thee bigge house ande didde have a verrie plesent tyme'. They sat in 'mye ladies little parler, a verrie fyne roome wyth sum grande chares ande littel tables' and 'her owne futman' waited on them. Then Lady Susan played some very pretty tunes on her spinet and told them that 'thee ladies in Lundun towne doe die their hayre, butt shee nott bein one two follow the fasshon, her owne was thee same as evver' and she remained 'a verrie sweete ladie ande nott a bitte uppish'. His lordship was less attractive. 'I fere hee doe care for noute butt hys dogges ande cup, I lyke nott hys ruffe wayes,' Anne wrote. 'Hee once trying toe kiss mee I didd boxe hys eres rite soundlie, att wyche hee was soe taken abacke, hee didde walke off rubbinge hys eers. I must wache Sarah that she cums nott in hys waye,' she added, 'shee bein a prettie wenche.'

Sarah's welfare was her constant concern. The girl came from a very poor but clean cottage on the farmer's property and was wonderfully grateful for the kindness and consideration she received from her mistress. She milked the cows and fed the hens, helped with the hay and was better at managing the bull than anyone else on the farm. She learnt to cook and not to pick up the chicken bones in her fingers when she was hungry; and when John's mother gave her a 'a silver peece ande a clene shifte wyth lase uppon it as well as a goode brown cloke ande a nite rail', she was so excited she burst into tears. If she was sometimes to be found in the cow-byre kissing and giggling with the carter's lad, she was always sorry afterwards and said she would rather stay with her mistress than get wed. Once, however, she went off to the stableyard at midnight 'to soe Hempseede' where the carter's boy would walk the next morning, in the fond hope that 'hys bigge feete crumpinge itt thee smell there off woulde reache hys nose ande soe make hym toe turne toe her from all thee other wenches'. In fact, he did not— he went out walking with Bella Griffin, the boldest of all the village girls and they were seen 'standeinge besydes a gaite agiggelinge'.

But a far happier and more romantic fate was in store for Sarah, for in September, 'the newe Passon didd cum, a younge ladd off 20 yeres or soe', named Godfrey Cross. He preached 'a pleasant sermun' in church on the Sunday and came back to the farmhouse for dinner—'a roste goose stuffed wythe boyled egges ande swete appels wyche didd cum oute nice ande jouisy'—and was seen 'toe looke att Sarah verrie prettie', so that Anne feared he was 'muche strucke wythe her', as indeed he was. Everyone in the village liked the young parson; he was kind and gentle and took trouble with his parishioners, going from one cottage to another on his white cob and entering into their lives in a way that Parson Ellis had never done. They liked his mother, too, who came to the parsonage to look after him and was very friendly towards Sarah, 'bein muche taken wythe her moddeste wayes'. By Christmas, when Anne gave a big party with everyone dancing to the gay sound of the spinet before they fell to playing 'Popp, bobbie appel ande snapp-dragon', Parson Cross was 'burninge hys fingers mitilie toe gett Sarah's plum', and her mistress realized that sooner or later she would have to 'loose' her maid.

The parson's mother got married first to a well-to-do tradesman called Master Jacob, living some twenty miles away, and by midsummer it was Sarah's turn. 'Sarah hav gott all reddie ande plentie toe her linnen cheste,' Anne wrote, 'ande alsoe a goode stocke off boddie linnen whyche Johns mother didd make looke verrie fyne wythe lase shee didd make her selfe. Ande shee didd tell Sarah toe care allus for thee underpart ande keepe itt neet ande thee topp woulde sure toe keepe soe.' Mistress Prue made her 'wedden gowne from Cousin Neds sattin, trimmed wythe fyne lase att thee sleves ande throte', the squire gave her a guinea and John killed a lamb and a sucking-pig to be roasted for the wedding feast. Cousin Mattie cooked the hares in port wine and stuffed them with chopped herbs and cinnamon, Cousin Flo baked dozens of cakes filled with butter and sugar and raspberry jam, and there were ducks and capons, hams and apple-pies, all of which made 'a mitie brave show', with the best

forks and glasses, silver pepper-pots, salt-cellars and
candlesticks brought out for the occasion. John looked
'verrie smarte in hys beste velvet cloes' and Anne put on
her 'blew sylke wythe the yallow lase'.

'Every boddie didd cum toe thee churche toe see thee
wedden, ande itt over wee back home, all goen off well att
thee churche. Then thee feestinge didd begin. . . . All didd
ett ande drynk hartilie, ande John didd tell all toe drynke
thee helthe off thee bride ande groome ande all didd soe
wythe muche laffinge ande muche passinge off bottels
ande jugges. . . . Later cum all thee villidge fokes toe thee
hous shoutinge ande singinge ande sayinge goode lucke
toe bothe, ande John did fetch in sheppherd ande carter
toe take oute sum jugges off cyder ande muche bredd ande
cheese soe all coulde hav sum. . . . Then wee toe injoye
our selfes wythe dansing ande muche talkinge, there bein
30 in all att thee feeste. Johns mother didd make a grett
bowel of punshe ande broute in sayinge all must drynke toe
thee goode lucke off thee yung fokes just begennen lyfe
together. Soe eache off thee vissitors didd take a drynke
from thee bowel, ande Cousin Ned didd say that as hee
culdent wedd Sarah hee would wait for her dauter, att
whyche shee didd blush verrie rosie, but passon didd laffe
ande say "verrie well itt was a barginn then". Then
Sarah didd saye howe muche shee didd want toe still bee
wyth us, butt shee didd say slylie what culde shee doe
wyth passon soe pressen. Att whyche all didd clapp
handes ande agree. Itt bein late bye thys tyme everrie
boddie didd starte home, albeit sum a bit jerkie from soe
muche wine drinkinge, ande Master Ferris didd saye hee
was goin toe ride hys horse backards home for thee tayle
was more toe holde on toe ande soe stedie hym. John didd
kiss all thee ladies in spite off thee scratting ande smakinge.
Then they all agon.'

The feasting was over. Anne gave the bride '10 guineas
for her stocken . . . soe shee doe starte her new lyfe wythe

K

summat toe her pockitt' and devoutly hoped 'shee maye bee as happie a wiffe as I bee wythe a goode husbun ande a goode home.' But her own pleasure of writing in her 'littel booke' was at an end, for without Sarah she knew that she would have 'toe muche work toe doe toe rite agen'.

8

THE GOLDEN AGE *of* TASTE

LIFE IN THE country began to change, not only as a result of the Enclosure Acts, but through the innumerable Turnpike Acts passed by Parliament, which at last had some effect on improving and maintaining the major roads in the kingdom. It was high time that something was done, for travelling at the beginning of the century had been a nightmare. It was dangerous, difficult and exhausting. Merchants living in the towns and the cities and rich noblemen with estates in the country travelled from necessity, not for pleasure, and never in the winter if their journey could be avoided. Even royalty suffered acutely, for when Queen Anne decided to remove her Court from Windsor to Bath, it took her four days to get there. Six stout horses with strong muscle-power were required to drag her richly carved coach along the agonizing roads, that were 'so Rocky, unlevel and Narrow' over the Marlborough Downs, the heavy royal coach, with the somewhat heavy royal lady inside it, was in constant danger of overturning.

But what Queen Anne endured was nothing to the difficulties her subjects encountered. Some preferred riding on horseback—at least you could see where you were going and be independent, though the chances of losing your way on the lonely, unfenced roads or of being set upon by highwaymen and left half-dead in a thicket, put terror into the most courageous heart. Some, if they could afford it, hired a post-chaise with two horses, one of them ridden by a post-boy in a yellow jacket, who took them some miles along the road and then handed them over to another post-boy for the next stage of their journey. Others had to travel by stage-coach, a huge, lumbering vehicle, which carried six inside passengers and as many as could be fitted into the wicker basket behind. Progress was painfully slow. The coach proprietors—or undertakers as they were ominously called—advertised that they would accomplish the journey from London to Bath or from London to York in four days, 'If God Permits'; and the travellers had no alternative but to accept hour upon hour of torment inside the fusty, damp and evil-smelling box which carried them—with luck—to their journey's end, jolting and swaying over every rut and cobblestone on the way with a motion that made everyone feel exceedingly sick. Likewise they had to put up with drunken coachmen, rotten harness, vicious horses and doubtful inns, where they spent the night uneasily sleeping two or three together in a truckle-bed or dozing upright in a chair. It was not surprising if their only comfort was hot brandy and sugar.

But the new Road Acts authorizing toll-gates to be set up every fifteen miles or so along the main roads, multiplied; and by the time King George III ascended the throne in 1760, the turnpike system had been extended to cover a wide area, bringing a distinct improvement and mitigating some of the worst terrors of travelling. Coaches, whether private or public, were redesigned to give more comfort to the passengers. The old-fashioned leather curtains were replaced by glass windows, seats were cushioned and the whole vehicle being lighter and less cumbersome could be drawn by four, or sometimes only two, horses at a much greater speed: too fast for some people, for when the Liverpool 'Flying Machine' covered the journey of 206 miles to London in three days, it was thought that the passengers might suffer 'an affection of the brain through travelling with such celerity'. Grave doubts were also expressed by the conservative innkeepers since the longer the delays the more money they could earn from the travellers having plenty of time to eat a gargantuan meal or to crack a third or a fourth bottle if the coachman was willing to wait for them.

The taste for speed, however, developed rapidly in the 1770s and was further accelerated in 1784 by the revolution in public transport devised by John Palmer of Bath. The son of a well-to-do brewer and spermaceti merchant, who owned a theatre in Bath and a theatre in Bristol, Palmer was a young man of great ability, determination and drive. Impatient with the absurd delays of the Post Office in distributing letters through the antiquated system of post-boys riding alone and unarmed across the countryside, he conceived the brilliant idea of sending the mail by a fast coach travelling at night with an armed guard to discourage highway robbery, and four inside passengers, whose fares would help to defray the cost.

Of course, the Post Office demurred, objecting strongly to any outside interference or investigation into their own incompetent bureaucratic behaviour, but when William Pitt came into power at the age of twenty-four, he over-ruled all the arguments of their Lordships the Postmasters-General and insisted on the experiment being put into operation at Palmer's own expense.

The first mail-coach left Bristol at four o'clock in the afternoon and reached London precisely on schedule at eight o'clock the next morning, and within a year or two the new system was so successful and so brilliantly organized by Palmer that it was extended to cover all the major towns in England and Scotland. A special coach was designed with an elegant body painted maroon and black, with scarlet wheels and the royal coat of arms embossed on the doors. The guards and the coachmen wore scarlet coats and top-hats, the guard sitting on the boot at the back with his feet on top of the locked mail-box and blowing his horn loud enough to wake the dead when the coach came within sight of a toll-gate. Infinite trouble was taken 'to keep the duty regular' and, in fact, the time-keeping was so good that people in the villages learnt to set their clocks by the mail, besides running out to wave and cheer as the coach swept along the road. When it stopped for a while for the horses to be changed and the mail-bags delivered, they crowded round it in excited admiration. No longer was one place isolated from another or from news of what was going on elsewhere; no longer were people of the middling sort, the tradesmen, well-to-do farmers and professional men of the smaller towns and villages, cut off from the world outside their own neighbourhood. Travelling had come within their reach, travelling for pleasure was at last a possibility, and the social consequences were more profound than anyone realized.

In the 1750s Thomas Turner, a mercer and general

dealer in the village of East Hoathly in Sussex, was entirely dependent on his neighbours for amusement and this meant playing cards, eating huge meals and drinking until he was fuddled, though he frequently reproached himself afterwards for behaving 'like an ass and in a way unworthy of a Christian'. The parson of the parish, Mr Porter, egged him on. After a supper consisting of four boiled chickens, four boiled ducks, minced veal, cold roast goose, chicken pasties and ham, with the parson and 'a mixed multitude', he wrote: 'Our behaviour was far from that of serious, harmless mirth, it was downright obstreperius. Our diversion was dancing and jumping about without a violin or any music, singing of foolish healths and drinking all the time as fast as it could be poured down.' And on another occasion the parson arrived at Turner's shop at six o'clock in the morning, 'drew me out of bed, but however permitted me to put on my breeches and instead of my upper cloaths gave me time to put on my wife's petticoats, and in this manner made me dance about till they had emptied a bottle of wine and also a bottle of ale'—all of which shamed him in his more sober moments later in the afternoon, so that once again he resolved to be more abstemious. Mrs Turner did not help him much—if anything she was rather worse than he was. She stayed at one rowdy party, after her husband had already slipped away, until five o'clock in the morning and had to be carried home pick-a-back by a servant.

Ten or twenty years later the Turners might have found less bibulous entertainment by travelling farther afield and mixing with a wider circle of acquaintances, for although the habit of drinking heavily was widespread among all classes, not everyone indulged in it to excess. Parson Woodforde was not like Parson Porter. He liked his food and his wine, but seldom did more than give himself the colic from over-eating and never drank to the extent of becoming indecent. When the farmers of Weston came to pay their tithes to him, he gave them six bottles of wine, a gallon and a half of rum and 'I know not what ale' and listened to the many droll songs they sang afterwards without attempting to drink more than a glass or two himself.

Woodforde was thirty-six when he settled at Weston Longeville in Norfolk and he lived there until his death in 1803; but his journeys down to Somerset to visit his relations and the sightseeing he did in London and in Bath on the way, enlarged his experience of life outside his own parish. He was not, like so many of the country clergy, ill-educated or too badly off. He went to Winchester and Oxford, where he was ordained and got his degree before returning home to Somerset as curate in his father's parish of Castle Cary. At Weston he kept a staff of two maidservants, two men and a boy and had his niece Nancy to look after him, so he had plenty of leisure to go fishing or hunting with Squire Custance, though once when they were out coursing a hare, he suddenly remembered that he was due to bury a dead parishioner at half past four in the afternoon and quickly had to ride back to the church in the middle of the hunt. Apart from this and one or two other lapses of memory, he generally took his duties quite seriously and was very charitable to the poor. At Christmas, besides giving money away, he sent 'the four Breasts and Hands of my two Piggs, with one of the Loins' to some of the poor families in the village and 'a good plate of rost Veal' to Tom Thurston's sick wife; and with an income of little more than £400 a year, he succeeded in entertaining his friends to some very good dinners at the parsonage. When he gave a summer party for the Squire and Mrs Custance and one other guest, he had 'a Couple of Chickens boiled and a Tongue, a Leg of Mutton boiled and Capers and Batter Pudding for the first Course; a Couple of Ducks rosted and green Peas, some Artichokes, Tarts and Blancmange

Mr and Mrs Garrick taking tea upon the lawn of their villa at Hampton by Johann Zoffany, *c.* 1760

Conversation Piece: A music party at home, *c.* 1720

A Cricket Match at Mousely Hurst, *c.* 1790

A Hunting Scene by John Wootton, *c.* 1740

Southwark Fair by William Hogarth, 1733

Vincent Lunardi's First Balloon Ascent from the Artillery Ground, London, in 1784

Exhibition of the Royal Academy in 1787

The Steine at Brighton in 1789 by Thomas Rowlandson

for the Second; and after dinner Almonds and Raisons, Oranges and Strawberries, the first gathered this year by me'. The Squire and his lady were very agreeable; 'they appeared to have had enough,' Woodforde observed, 'and were very well pleased and merry.'

It was only poor Nancy who sometimes got rather bored at Weston. It was not that she did not enjoy the society of Mrs Custance and the rest of the neighbours; it was that she missed her sisters and her brothers and all her young cousins in Somerset. Her uncle was kind enough. He gave her 'a brown silk gown trimmed with Furr' made from a very good rich silk which had belonged to his Aunt Parr, and she wore it when she went to Norwich with Mrs Davy, though Woodforde did not quite approve of her friendship with this rather giddy widowed lady. In a weak moment of fun, he once stole one of Mrs Davy's garters and kept it, but when he thought Nancy was learning some extravagant notions from her, he lectured his niece severely; perhaps the garter was on his conscience, or perhaps Mrs Davy was too familiar. Having no home of her own, she was continually at the parsonage, sometimes staying for weeks on end with her daughter Betsy, or taking Nancy off to her lodgings at Hockering, until finally poor Woodforde, having heard some scandalous gossip about the Davys and being 'almost continually vexed and tormented' by Nancy's connexion with them, sent his servant over in his little cart to fetch her home at once. Betsy's young man, Walker, proved to be 'the most profligate, wicked, artful, ungrateful and deceiving wretch, and', wrote Woodford, 'I believe both Mother Davy and her Daughter also to be very cunning, close and not without much Art'. So that was that; Nancy had to abide by her uncle's opinion and drop their acquaintance.

Nancy used the little market-cart quite a lot for short journeys around the countryside; otherwise she had to ride pillion behind her uncle or his manservant, or wait

for the Squire and Mrs Custance to send their coach for
her. To hire a chaise for going into Norwich was somewhat expensive; it cost 15s, which was more than
Woodforde could afford except when they set off with all
their luggage for the long journey down to Somerset.
This was quite an undertaking. They usually went in the
night-coach from Norwich to London, spent two or three
days sightseeing there and then went on via Salisbury, or
sometimes via Bath, to Cole, where Woodforde's Sister
Pouncett, as he always called her, lived with her husband.
In London their favourite inn was the Bell Savage on
Ludgate Hill and this in spite of the fact that whenever
he stayed there, Woodforde was always 'bit terribly by the
Buggs in the night' and had to resort to sitting up in a
chair fully dressed to avoid them.

The 'Buggs' did not seem to bother Nancy. She had a
wonderful time. She went to the Tower of London and
saw the wild beasts, the regalia and 'the Horse Armory',
watched the changing of the guard in St James's Park and
went to the Royal Mews, where she sat in the King's state
coach and saw his cream-coloured horses. She went to the
circus in St George's Fields and to a play at the Little
Theatre in the Haymarket, had her hair 'full dressed' in
the Strand at her uncle's expense and did a lot of shopping
in Covent Garden, buying 'Gauze Gloves, Ribbands and
lace' at Charlesworth's, an elegant mercer's in Tavistock
Street and '3 dressed Caps' at a milliner's near by. They
dined every day at the 13 Cantons in Charing Cross on
beef *à la mode* and frequently refreshed themselves on rum
and water or by drinking tea in a respectable coffee house;
and it was great fun for Nancy when her brother Bill, who
was in the Navy, travelled with them. One evening the two
young people gave their uncle the slip and went out on
their own, not returning until supper-time. Woodforde
was hurt and 'much displeased' by their behaviour,
though he forgave them the next morning.

Bill was a gay young man, somewhat irresponsible in his uncle's opinion. He went off with a friend of his and nearly missed the Bath coach, returning only just in time before it was due to start off at seven o'clock in the evening. It was called the 'Balloon Coach' in honour of the first balloon ascent made by an enterprising young Italian called Vincent Lunardi, and was even faster and more elegant than the mail-coach, travelling down to the fashionable west-country resort in record time. Here again Nancy enjoyed herself, visiting the Pump Room and the Assembly Rooms for the first time and being tempted by the modish shops in Milsom Street. They spent the night at the Castle Inn and at noon the next day hired a post-chaise to take them to Shepton Mallet and from there another post-chaise on to Cole, where Woodforde's Sister Pouncett was delighted to see them and Nancy was reunited with her young cousins. Her father and mother, two aunts and another uncle all lived around Ansford and Castle Cary and they all had children of varying ages who made Nancy's life much more amusing than it was at Weston Parsonage, so that when she got back to Norfolk again, her uncle wrote sadly: 'My niece hath been almost daily making me uneasy by continually complaining of the dismal Life she leads at Weston Parsonage for want of being out more in Company and having more at home.' But there was nothing much he could do about it; he could not afford the long journey down to Somerset every year and by the time he had saved enough money to buy a chaise of his own, he did not feel well enough to go so far.

Well-off people now took to making tours round the country during the summer months, travelling hundreds of miles in their own carriages to visit their friends and relations and putting up at the inns along the road. Some of the accommodation was appalling, but Mrs Lybbe Powys of Hardwick House in Oxfordshire did not mind that. 'The pleasures of travelling in my opinion ever compensate for inconveniences on the road,' she wrote, adding rather smugly: 'Ladies too delicate should remain at their own seats.' Quite undaunted by the distance, she took her six-year-old son, little Phil, all the way to Ludlow to stay with some of her husband's relations and since her husband disliked maidservants fussing about on a journey, with only one manservant in attendance. They travelled in their own carriage as far as Benson and then in post-chaises, being 'more expeditious than coach or phaeton', through Oxford, Broadway and Pershore to Worcester, arriving there in the moonlight, 'neither ourselves nor our little companion in the least fatigued'.

Worcester was a charming city, 'in some parts well built with a fine assembly room and an excellent town-hall'; the cathedral was 'indifferent', but the china factory a great novelty, because it employed more than 160 people, a vast number of them small boys not much older than little Phil. The Powys relations lived twenty-five miles away on the road to Ludlow in a large house with a splendid view of the surrounding country and their manner of living, 'blended with every elegance and fashionable taste', was open-handed and generous. There were hordes of servants both indoors and out to ensure the comfort and the leisure of the household—the little girls aged five and ten, each had a separate maid; and the house party never numbered less than twenty to say nothing of the guests from round about, who came in for dinner almost every day and went off shooting in the park or racing at Ludlow. 'Two lords and six baronets with their families' attended the race-assembly in Ludlow, the ladies wearing all their finest jewels and dancing until five o'clock in the morning, besides patronizing the theatre where a special company of actors had assembled for the occasion. Little Phil enjoyed himself hugely and was a tremendous success. 'Three or four times a day he acted

Prince Henry to audiences of 20 or 30 people with vast *éclat*. Luckily he don't mind strangers,' his mother wrote proudly. 'I think shy children of his age are dreadful.'

On the way home the Powys family did some sight-seeing, visiting Lord Hertford's seat at Ragley and Mr Martin's at Overbury, and passing many other beautiful houses before they reached their own, set 'in the sweet softness and natural simplicity of the wooded valley of the Thames'. What they and the other energetic tourists of this time saw was a country more beautiful than it had ever been before or would ever be again, for this was the golden age of England's aesthetic development. Nature had been tamed by the gentle art of man, not yet wilfully destroyed for the sake of mammon. Agricultural progress since the enclosure of the land had created green pastures and opulent fields of corn where once there had been acres of scrub on the rough commons, while the mania of the cultured aristocracy for building and for redesigning their parks and gardens had brought a new harmony into the landscape. Pope's dictum 'to consult the genius of the place' had not been forgotten; and although the nobility derived their inspiration from the paintings of Claude and the classical architecture of Palladio, they assimilated both these foreign influences into a style of their own, which gave English houses and English gardens of the eighteenth century a grace and a loveliness never to be surpassed or equalled anywhere in the world.

Many of the rich landowners intent on improving their estates were animated by the desire to show off, yet at no other time had they ever been so personally involved in the pleasure of creating a superb setting for themselves and their families, and their taste was well-nigh flawless. At Holkham, young Thomas Coke, later Earl of Leicester, reclaimed hundreds of acres of bleak and windswept salt-marshes on the Norfolk coast and through his own expert knowledge of horticulture, transformed the unlovely countryside into a noble park and garden. Soon afterwards, with the assistance of Lord Burlington and William Kent, he started building a spacious Palladian mansion, becoming so absorbed in the study of architecture that it was 'his chief amusement and delight during the greatest part of his life'. No detail was too small to be given his personal attention and no expense was spared on the continual process of improving and perfecting Kent's original plans. The interior was sumptuous and ornate with long vistas from one room to another, coffered ceilings, marble columns and carved chimney-pieces, yet restrained by the Earl of Leicester's own feeling for the classical proportion of one space in relation to another and his flair for composing a magnificent setting for the paintings, statuary and rare books he had started collecting on the Grand Tour and could never resist adding to as the years went on.

Mrs Lybbe Powys, on one of her sightseeing tours in 1756, thought the gallery at Holkham, 'painted dead white with ornamental gilding, the most superbly elegant room' she had ever seen. But by then, in spite of the ever-increasing number of his treasured possessions, which included a notebook of Leonardo da Vinci's, Rubens's 'Holy Family', a splendid Van Dyck and several paintings by Claude, the Earl himself was a disappointed man. His only son, a pretty boy and a sensitive youth, had turned into a vicious, dissolute young man and was now dead without having provided a legitimate heir. Kent and Burlington, who had shared his intellectual and artistic tastes when he was young and full of enthusiasm, were also dead. There was no one left to appreciate or to inherit the glory of Holkham, except a nephew whom the Earl did not care for, and none of his treasures could compensate for this. The tablet he had proudly raised over the portico of his palatial house stating that 'This seat, on an open barren estate, was planned, planted, built, decorated and inhabited in the middle of the VIIIth century by Thos. Coke, Earl of Leicester' was a mocking witness to his disenchantment.

At Stourhead, Henry Hoare, a grandson of the founder of Hoare's Bank, was more fortunate—at the age of eighty he was still enjoying the glorious landscape garden he had planned and planted in Wiltshire. Indeed, long before the term landscape gardening had been applied to the English scene, this brilliant though unassuming amateur, anticipating the work of Lancelot Brown and Humphrey Repton, had achieved a masterpiece, described by Horace Walpole as 'one of the most picturesque scenes in the world'. His father had bought the neglected estate of the Stourton family in 1720 and having demolished the old baronial mansion, had built himself a modern house in the Palladian manner, which was finished only just before he died five years later. The site chosen for the new house lay to the north of an irregular valley surrounded by high barren hills where a few skinny sheep nibbled at the rough pasture and where Henry Hoare, as a young man fresh from his travels in Italy, saw his vision of a Claudian landscape out in the open air, made three-dimensional by nature's own florescence and the luminous light of the sky.

'He had the good taste and the good sense not to call in the assistance of a professional gardener. He saw with his own eyes and suggested improvements with his own hands'; and the first thing he did was to build a dam at the south-west corner of the valley to form a large lake covering a space of twenty acres. Round the steep sides of the lake he planted beech-trees and firs, cedars from North America and other exotics from as far away as China, composing an idyllic panorama of trees and water, which he then embellished at significant points with a series of classical temples, a romantic grotto, a stone bridge and a medieval cross. As in Claude's spacious and tranquil compositions, art and nature were fused into a classical-romantic conception of flawless beauty, unfolding like the pastoral poems of Virgil in a magic cadence of sylvan groves, melting distances and temples reflected in the shining surface of the lake. There was nothing at Stourhead to hurt the eye or to disrupt the mood of quiet contemplation. Henry Hoare's unerring instinct for the lyrical and lovely landscape that he had dreamed of as a young man of great wealth with leisure enough to pursue his ideal, was fulfilled in his own lifetime; and as he grew older 'he had the satisfaction of hearing his own creation universally admired and of seeing a barren waste covered in luxuriant woods'.

Mrs Lybbe Powys, sightseeing again in her indefatigable way, preferred Stourhead to Stowe, though the famous gardens there had been laid out originally by Queen Caroline's gardener, Bridgeman, the inventor of the ha-ha ditch which brought the countryside into the view of the unfenced garden without a break, and greatly enhanced by the temples and other ornaments designed by Vanbrugh and Gibbs for the first Lord Cobham in the early years of the century. Not content with this arrangement, Cobham also employed Kent to develop the Elysian Fields and the Grecian Valley, and was the first of the affluent Whig lords to promote the interests of Lancelot Brown, then a very young man working in the kitchen garden at Stowe. Kent's genius for softening the more formal layout of Bridgeman and his superb taste in designing suitable buildings to enrich his idealized landscape, had a marked influence on Brown, who presently moved to Hammersmith to set up on his own, becoming in the 1760s and the 1770s 'the much sought after Mr Brown', called 'Capability' from his habit of viewing an estate and talking of its capabilities.

He came of humble Northumbrian parents and was educated at the village school in Kirkharle; and even

when his work was earning him a fortune and he was
accepted as a celebrity in the highest circles of the
aristocracy, he remained simple in his tastes and enjoyed
most of all being at home with 'his dear, faithful and
affectionate wife' Bridget and their children. Not that he
ever had much time to be with his family or any leisure at
his command; he was constantly travelling round the
country to give his advice and often torn between two or
more landowners clamouring for his attention. They found
in him a man of integrity and truth, always good-
humoured and with a purpose exactly in accord with their
own liberal ideas of naturalizing and improving their
property. For Brown went even further than Kent; he
aimed to create a gentle serenity within the natural features
of the landscape and succeeded brilliantly in the ravishing
green turf reaching to the serpentine lake that no great
garden of his design could be without, in the noble
clumps of trees shading the speckled deer within the
boundaries of the park and in the subtle views he revealed
of the distant horizon.

At Longleat he swept away the clipped alleys and
formal parterres of Lord Weymouth's seventeenth-century
forbears and in doing so somewhat shocked Mrs Delany
when she returned there on a visit in 1760. 'There is not
much alteration to the house,' she wrote, 'but *the gardens
are no more!* They are succeeded by a fine lawn, a serpentine river, wooded hills, gravel paths meandering round a
shrubbery, *all modernised* by the ingenious and much
sought after *Mr Brown!*' But Lord Weymouth himself was
highly delighted, she reported, and 'so fond of the place
that he leaves it with reluctance'; and Brown's success at
Longleat was repeated on countless other estates as far
apart as Croome Court near Worcester, Cardiff Castle and
Harewood House in Yorkshire. The beauty of the English
landscape, of park and garden blending with the hills and
the valleys of the green countryside, owed more to him

than to any other individual. He had his followers and his imitators and there were others besides Mrs Delany who accused him of ruthlessly destroying the great gardens of his predecessors; but after his death, Horace Walpole wrote: 'His great and fine genius stood unrivalled; and it was the peculiar felicity of it that it was allowed by all ranks and degrees of society. . . . Those who knew him best or practised near him, were not able to determine whether the quickness of his eye, or its correctness were most to be admired. It was comprehensive and elegant, and perhaps it may be said never to have failed him.'

Meanwhile elegance in architecture was entering a new phase and, while 'Capability' Brown was redesigning the landscape, Robert Adam and his brother James, the sons of a Scottish architect, had returned from a tour of Rome and the Adriatic with a portfolio of drawings that were exciting and imaginative and with an introduction from Lady Wortley Montagu to her son-in-law, Lord Bute. Robert had studied the palace of Diocletian at Spalatro, Piranesi's picturesque engravings of *Roma Antica,* the new archaeological discoveries at Herculaneum and Pompeii and the paintings in the Etruscan tombs of the Roman countryside; and from these diverse elements, he created a style of his own that was highly personal, more delicate and less static than the classical Palladian form and based on his own distinctive theory of movement in architecture having 'the same effect that hill and dale, foreground and distance, swelling and sinking, have in landscape'.

Lord Bute, the favourite of King George III and his dominating mother, the dowager Princess Augusta, was not very sympathetic towards his young fellow-country-man. He was 'booted and spurred' when he received him and cut the interview short, so that Adam was furious. 'I have a great mind,' he told a friend, 'to go out to Kensington and when My Lord and Madame la Princesse are stewing together, I'll have them put in a boat naked and brought down the river like Adam and Eve and I'll fell him dead with Piranesi's four-folio volumes from Westminster Bridge!' Happily there were others among the rich and fashionable *cognoscenti* in London who were more appreciative of the ambitious young architect's brilliant drawings, and although most of them went away expressing their admiration without offering to pay for the designs they asked him for, it was not long before he found a distinguished patron in Sir Nathaniel Curzon of Kedleston Hall in Derbyshire. Sir Nathaniel was 'struck all of a heap with wonder and amaze' by the drawings Adam showed him, and his wife Lady Caroline, 'excessively beautiful and free of pride and affectation', was equally enthusiatic. It was a little unfortunate that Matthew Brettingham had already been invited to work on Kedleston, but this problem was overcome and by 1763 Adam was in Derbyshire supervising the erection of the south front in a manner that was 'highly skilled and vastly original'. All the elements were classical, but all the parts advanced, receded and flowed into each other, the outward curve of the dome contrasting with the concave curve of the double flight of entrance steps and the pedimental door set within a shallow, arched recess, a motif Adam was often to repeat in his later and more mature style.

The mastery he showed at Kedleston set him off on a career, which became phenomenally successful all through the 1760s and the 1770s. Harewood House in Yorkshire, Saltram House in Devon, Mersham-le-Hatch in Kent, Osterley, Syon, Kenwood and Garrick's villa at Hampton were all built, extended or remodelled to his designs; even the conceited, high-handed and perverse Lord Bute invited him to work at Luton Hoo. And like Kent before him, though with a far lighter and more delicate touch, Adam was responsible for all the interior decorations of the houses he planned, from the graceful swags of flowers, wreaths, vases and medallions ornamenting the walls and the ceilings, down to the smallest detail in the exquisitely wrought brass handles and escutcheons on the doors. A team of cabinet-makers—Chippendale, Linnell, France and Hepplewhite; of artists such as Antonio Zucchi, Angelica Kauffmann, Cipriani and Bonomi; of carpet-weavers and fabric-workers in damask, brocade and satin, all contributed to the perfection of his requirements, which were 'to seize . . . the beautiful spirit of antiquity and to transform it with novelty and variety fit for an English gentleman's house'.

Visiting Osterley in the 1770s, Horace Walpole was enchanted with the hall, library, breakfast-room and eating-room, and with 'a drawing-room worthy of Adam and Eve before the Fall'; but he disliked the Etruscan Room 'painted all over like Wedgwood's ware with black and yellow small grotesques'. Adam himself strongly defended this as 'a mode of Decoration differing from anything practised in Europe' and he was constantly developing and improving his schemes with a freshness and a diversity that astonished his patrons. At Kenwood, the new owner Lord Mansfield, appointed Lord Chief Justice in 1756, gave full scope to his ideas and being immensely rich, never questioned the cost; and for the library, with its curved ceiling leading into two apsidal ends screened by pairs of fluted columns, Adam designed one of the most harmonious and elegant rooms he had yet conceived, intimate in scale and rich, though not gaudy, in decoration. The delicate plaster ornaments on the ceiling were executed by Joseph Rose and the paintings in the centre oval and the surrounding lunettes by Zucchi, who sent in a bill for 'Tableaux peints pour Son Excellence My Lord Mansfield' for £152 5s. Chippendale supplied the mirrors to the architect's own minutely detailed specification at a cost of £340, and William

France put in an account for £12 7s 6d for providing '2 very elegant Screens richly carved and gilded . . . as also the Ornaments very perfectly carved in good shape . . . and for Covering the Screen Parts with White Cloth and fine Elephant paper and your own India Damask'; with '2 Crimson Serge Cases to the 2 Screens above at £1 9s and a man carrying Do to Kenwood, 2s.'

Lord Mansfield, a great scholar and a friendly host, made Kenwood his permanent home after the mob in the 'No Popery' riots of 1780 had destroyed his other residence in Bloomsbury Square and were only prevented from setting fire to Kenwood as well by the landlord of the near-by Spaniards Inn filling the rioters up with so much liquor that they were incapable of moving on. The house stood in the still unspoilt country on the rural fringe of London, near enough to the city for his guests to ride out for a day's enjoyment in the sweet air of Hampstead—among them, David Garrick, one of Lord Mansfield's oldest friends, who as early as 1757 had himself been seeking a country house not too far from London, where he could enjoy some leisure from the incessant turmoil of his life in the theatre. Not Hampstead but Hampton, overlooking a glistening reach of the Thames close to Hampton Court, was his final choice; and since besides being a great actor at the height of his glory, he was ever anxious to cut an imposing figure in the fashionable world off the stage, he naturally employed both 'Capability' Brown and Robert Adam to convert his property into a country seat 'fit for a gentleman'.

Adam put an elegant new front on the old house with 'an Arcade and a Portico and a Pediment over, and stone Pilasters and Cornice corresponding'; and 'Capability' Brown solved the problem of the riverside lawn being separated from the house by a main road in the same way that Pope had solved a similar problem at Twickenham, by making a grotto beneath the road with a rusticated arch at either end and a highly convenient bath-house supplied by a spring of excellent water. On the Thames lawn Garrick built a Temple to Shakespeare and here, with his wife Eva-Maria and his intimate friends, he enjoyed the Arcadian prospect of the swans gliding on the gleaming water and the weeping-willows for ever gazing at their own reflection. As if to convince himself that all this was not too good to be true for the boy from Lichfield with his patched coat and empty pockets, he commissioned a very young artist, Johann Zoffany, to capture the idyllic scene on canvas and, in doing so, started Zoffany off on a successful career which took him from one country house to another to record the life of leisure and pleasure enjoyed by the landed gentry and their families on their own estates.

For Garrick was not alone in being proud of himself and his property, or in wishing to perpetuate the gracious manner of living which he and so many of the country gentlemen he imitated had achieved by the middle of the century. The Conversation Piece in painting, showing an informal group of the family out of doors or at home in the drawing-room, was already highly esteemed and had been practised with some success by Hogarth in his early years, by his friend Francis Hayman, by Arthur Devis and many other English or Anglicized artists. Gainsborough's first commissions, before he moved from Suffolk to Bath in 1759, were all of figures in a landscape. His portrait of Mr and Mrs Andrews sitting on a rustic bench in the cool shade of an oak-tree by a ripening field of corn glowing in the golden light of a summer evening, was a marvellous evocation of the young couple's pleasure in the sensuous beauty of their surroundings; and the same subtle atmosphere of quiet content appeared again in his view of the Lloyd children resting in a 'Capability' Brown landscape of lake and trees under a luminous sky. Indeed, it was Gainsborough's 'strong inclination for Landskip' that first encouraged him to take up painting and the vivid light of his native East Anglia that inspired him as it was later to inspire Constable. The spontaneity of his vision and his naturalism were as new to painting as Brown's approach to the art of gardening and never more freely expressed than in the lyrical association of figures and natural scenery in his early work.

It was against his inclination and because he needed money that Gainsborough forced himself to become a portrait-painter of fashionable society after moving to Bath and even then, in contrast to Reynolds's rhetorical style, he insisted on showing his sitters against the background of an imaginary landscape, which blended with their mood of the moment and became an integral part of the overall design. 'Nothing can be more absurd than the foolish custom of painters dressing people in fancy dress and expecting the likeness to appear,' he wrote; and again, in direct opposition to his great rival's theory or heroic portraiture: 'I have that regard for truth that I hold the finest inventions as a mere slave in comparison, and believe I shall remain an ignorant fellow to the end of my days, because I never could have patience to read poetical impossibilities, the very food of a painter, especially if he intends to be knighted in this land of roast beef, so well do serious people love froth.'

Impatience with his fashionable sitters often drove Gainsborough to fury, though even when they did not understand him or his brilliant handling of paint in the flickering, feathery brush-strokes he used for his later work, they were usually satisfied with the likeness he caught. Even Reynolds had to admit that the unfinished appearance of some of his canvases, by allowing the spectator to use his imagination, contributed more to the striking resemblance which made his portraits so remarkable than a more obvious and conventional pictorial technique would have done. But the sitters themselves were more concerned with their social dignity, with the pride of being painted by an artist who was considered by some to be even greater than Sir Joshua and worthy of a place among the family portraits of their ancestors. The ladies were beautiful—no one but Gainsborough ever made them look so beautiful; the gentlemen were unmistakably aristocratic and not at all unwilling to show themselves off in their elegant youth or in the splendour of their maturity.

The gentlemen had, in fact, already taken the lead in stimulating the Englishness of English art in another direction through their desire to be seen among their favourite dogs and horses out hunting, or with their guns and their gamekeepers on some recognizable part of their estates. For them the Conversation Piece was not enough; it was small in scale, not big enough, not grand enough to satisfy their overwhelming instinct for the pleasure they derived from hunting and shooting. So in the 1720s the 3rd Duke of Beaufort sent John Wootton to Rome to study the landscapes of Claude and Poussin and when he returned, commissioned him to paint five enormous pictures of the stag-hunting, the hare-hunting and the horse-racing at Badminton. These large canvases were so successful that Lord Weymouth invited Wootton to Longleat to paint a similar series to hang in the great hall among the sporting trophies and armorial bearings of his ancestors. Other artists, James Seymour and the Anglicized Pieter Tillemans worked for the Duke of Norfolk, the Duke of Richmond and Earl Spencer of Althorp, painting their hounds and their huntsmen with more freedom from the foreign influences absorbed by Wootton; and in the second half of the century, George Stubbs, after studying anatomy in York, established himself as the most sought after animal-painter of his day.

He was more gifted and more sensitive than any of the other artists working as sporting-painters. All nature was his field and, although he was largely self-taught, he had a brilliant sense of colour and a highly developed pictorial imagination. The horses, the hunt servants and the hounds he painted for the pleasure of his noble patrons were represented with absolute fidelity in the clear light of the countryside; for Stubbs, like Gainsborough in his youth, saw the English landscape through English eyes and refused to be led astray by the foreign paintings in the grand manner so highly prized by the *cognoscenti*. When he travelled in Italy, it was not as he said, 'to study art, but to prove to himself that this was unnecessary. He had no use for the pompous ideology of the sublime and the antique so strongly advocated by Sir Joshua at the Royal Academy. He believed, on the contrary, that 'nature was superior to art', thereby emphasizing the new trend in taste veering away from the classical towards the romantic —an ideal which was to become the passion and the pleasure of the younger generation growing up at the end of the century.

9

ROMANTIC PASSIONS

THE ELEGANT TASTE of the aristocracy, classical in origin yet more and more romantic in feeling, not only had a profound and lasting effect on the landscape of England, but on the appearance of her old-established towns and cities, where people of the middling sort lived and worked and were now enjoying more prosperity than they had ever known before. Much of the land in London and elsewhere was owned by the nobility and developed by them in conjunction with their favourite architects, or with speculative builders working to a coherent design which preserved all the elements of order, dignity and proportion to be seen in the great country houses. Thus whole areas were transformed by new streets of terraced houses in brick with stone dressings, sash-windows and fanlights over the front door, or in squares set round a central space of trees and lawns deliberately suggesting a landscape garden in miniature. The handsome Palladian crescents in Bath enfolding a panorama of the city, were copied at Cheltenham, Scarborough and Buxton, and even the expanding industrial towns of the North and the

160

Midlands were not yet the dark and overcrowded eyesores that they would one day become. Of the 12,000 houses registered in Birmingham in 1790, 8,000 had been built since 1760 in a good plain style, mainly to accommodate the skilled workers, whose 'art and industry had already made the town famous all over the world for all sorts of wares and curiosities in iron, steel, brass etc., admired as well for their cheapness as their peculiar beauty of workmanship'. Mr Turner's Brassworks and the other factories which gave so much opportunity to the men of inventive genius like James Watt and Matthew Boulton, had not yet eaten up the surrounding country. Farms and fields were within easy reach of Manchester and Derby also, and at Newcastle, though their hours were long and hard and their work was highly dangerous, the coal-miners had the Town Moor where they could forgather as pigeon fanciers or to gamble on the horse-racing and prize-fighting.

Town planning had never before reached such a high peak of aesthetic achievement and was never to do so again. People of the middling sort who belonged to this period of urban development, the lawyers, doctors, tradesmen, craftsmen and shopkeepers, absorbed the civilized taste of their environment as the air itself. There was no pleasure they or their wives enjoyed more than aping their betters, nothing they were more proud of than the increasing gentility of their domestic lives. If they were not born in the top drawer, at least they could live in a town house or a villa in the suburbs built to the designs published by Colen Campbell or the Adam brothers, and have furniture about them copied from the patterns in Chippendale's *Gentleman's and Cabinet-Maker's Director* or in Hepplewhite's *Cabinet-Maker and Up-holsterer's Guide*. The pottery of Mr Josiah Wedgwood with his Greek designs so artfully reproduced and hand-painted, was quite within their means, and even if

Dr Johnson did mock at their pretensions, many a grocer's wife could boast of a tea-table as well set up as any lady of quality; for the small factories producing elegant table-ware, the country craftsmen imitating the leading cabinet makers and the provincial silversmiths knew their job. Nothing was shoddy and nothing was ugly; mass production for commercial gain was still in its infancy.

'I had before discovered that there was nowhere but in England the distinction of *middling* people,' wrote Horace Walpole on returning from the Continent. 'I perceive now that there is peculiar to us *middling* houses; how snug they are!' Not only around his delightful Twickenham area, but in other parts of Middlesex and in Essex, especially around Epping, the country was dotted with villas built by prosperous city merchants, whose acquisition of more wealth and leisure had come about from the expansion of British trading overseas. Mr Hague of the East India Company had a villa at Watten-on-the-Forest, a handsome chariot of his own 'with a pair of fine nagtail bays' and two 'very genteel' servants as coachman and footman. If he did not actually belong to the landowning class, he had money enough to enjoy a high style of living and no shame at all when he travelled into the City through some of the stinking and derelict streets inhabited by the poor. Success was everything; it bought grace and comfort and satisfaction with a system of government which allowed an astute individual to prosper while contributing to the overall wealth of the nation.

The rewards of thrift, energy, inventive skill and a certain amount of sharp practice were very great in the 1770s and the 1780s. 'Men are every day starting up from obscurity to wealth,' Johnson declared; and it was possible for anyone with drive and persistence to rise from the middling sort to a position of power and affluence in the thriving industries of the North and the Midlands or in the ever-expanding financial complex of London. Many of the most successful merchant bankers and *nouveau-riche* industrialists bought themselves large estates in the country and aspiring to the high taste of the aristocratic *cognoscenti*, competed with them at Mr Christie's auction-rooms in Pall Mall for the works of art that came on the market; and if the genuine Guido Renis, Domenichinos, Raphaels and Titians were too expensive, they could get copies of them to adorn their walls painted or engraved by English artists. The snob value of the old masters, whether phoney or not, was considerable.

But for those with a more modest appetite for culture and a less well-filled purse, there were the new aquatints published by every bookseller and art-dealer around the country and the water colours and topographical drawings of a new generation of English artists, whose romantic approach to nature was entirely original. At first the drawings and water-colours of Paul Sandby, Thomas Malton and Edward Dayes were bought as souvenirs to remind people of the pictorial scenes they had become familiar with through the increased facilities they enjoyed for travelling about and sightseeing. Then, gradually, the view of nature revealed by these talented Englishmen, working in a medium that had long been despised, began to encourage a great number of people who had never really thought of looking at the countryside, to take pleasure in observing its beauties for themselves; and when other artists, like Francis Towne, Alexander and John Robert Cozens returned from travelling abroad, they learnt to look for something that Horace Walpole and his friend Gray had discovered on their first visit to the Continent—for the picturesque in nature and the awe-inspiring, romantic mystery of mountain scenery.

Many of the young Milords rattling across Europe in their private carriages with the classical glories of Rome and Naples as the object of their journey, could not help but feel a *frisson* of terror, some subconscious stirring of the emotions when they reached the Alps and beheld the fearful, frozen magnitude of nature's incomparable vastness for the first time. But Walpole and Gray were more sensitive than most and the impression lasted all their lives. Of their journey through the mountains of Savoy, Walpole wrote ecstatically to his friend Richard West: 'But the road, West, the road! winding round a prodigious mountain and surrounded with others, all shagged with hanging woods, obscured with pines or lost in clouds! Below, a torrent breaking through cliffs, and tumbling through fragments of rocks! Sheets of cascades forcing their silver speed down channelled precipices, and hasting into the roughened river at the bottom! Now and then an old foot-bridge, with a broken rail, a leaning cross, a cottage or the ruin of a hermitage! This sounds too bombast and romantic to one that has not seen it, too cold for one that has.' And to Gray there was 'not a precipice, not a torrent, not a cliff but is pregnant with religion and poetry'. The only equivalent experience he had was years later when he visited Blair Athol and exclaimed: 'Since I saw the Alps I have seen nothing sublime until now. The mountains are extatic, and ought to be visited in pilgrimage once a year. None but these monstrous creatures of God know how to join so much beauty with so much horror.'

Walpole, meanwhile, in defiance of the aristocratic taste of his friends, consistently pursued his own delight in the picturesque, a word he was the first to use and one which had not been included in Johnson's *Dictionary*. He admired the romantic paintings of Salvator Rosa, the heroic ballads in Percy's *Reliques of Ancient English Poetry*, published in 1765 and the high-flown translations of Gaelic poetry faked by Macpherson in his much discussed *Ossian*. He even wrote the first of the Gothic horror-novels soon to become so popular—*The Castle of Otranto*—and although he affected to despise it as 'a little thing' thrown off by an idle gentleman to amuse himself and endeavoured to excuse 'the wildness of the story', it made Gray, with whom he was now reconciled, 'cry a little . . . and afraid to go to bed o'nights'. It also influenced some years later the hectic imagination of the very rich, very wild and very eccentric young William Beckford, who in three days and three nights of feverish activity produced *The History of the Caliph Vathek,* a still more preposterous tale of horror with an oriental background of concupiscence that was a mark of his own adolescent frustration.

All his life, led on by the restless, romantic eroticism that obsessed him, Beckford failed to find any real satisfaction in the bizarre pleasures he pursued with such eagerness. He fell in love with a boy of twelve, was entangled with his cousin's wife, married and lost his own beautiful wife, and built his fantastic Gothic Abbey at Fonthill at such a pace and with so little attention to its solid structure that the tower twice fell down, collapsing in a heap of rubble. His perfumed couches, concealed celestial music, incense burning and quasi-religious black magic rites in the huge, draughty oratory of his Abbey were bound to disappoint him in the end, for nothing however exotic could ever match the sensational craving of his imagination and he could never quite live up to his own seductive conception of non-conformity. It was only in the extensive grounds of Fonthill, deliberately planted with firs and forest trees hanging to the hills and overshadowing the dark lake near the Abbey, very like the surroundings of the ancient monasteries he had seen in the Swiss Alps and in Portugal, that he came near to achieving a synthesis of his romantic emotions; and even then he was constrained to build a twelve-foot-high wall all round his estate to keep his fox-hunting neighbours out and his Gothic fantasy of beauty and horror for himself alone.

Neither Walpole nor Gray had the temperament or the means to follow his taste for romanticism with the enigmatic zeal of Beckford; but whereas both were highly susceptible to the pleasure of being roused by the wildness and the beauty of natural scenery, Dr Johnson, as might be expected, was not. He had no sympathy with the romantic ideal. His judgement on Gray as a poet was exceedingly harsh and his views on the poems of *Ossian* were unfavourable. The epic poem of Fingal, which enraptured so many people, was, he said, 'a mere unconnected rhapsody, a tiresome repetition of the same images', adding: 'In vain shall we look for the *lucidus ordo* where there is neither end or object, design or moral, *nec certa recurrit imago.*' He was rude also about the passion of his friend William Shenstone for landscape gardening, suggesting that 'to make water run where it will be heard and to stagnate where it will be seen, to leave intervals where the eye will be pleased and to thicken the plantations where there is something to be hidden . . . is rather the sport than the business of human reason.' Anything new which did not fit in with the old scholar's concept of reason, common sense and proportion, anything which upset his own egocentric principles of morality and wisdom, was, in fact, suspect. He was ageing rapidly and his circle of admirers was diminishing.

There were still Sir Joshua and Boswell and Edmund Burke when he was not drowning in his own brilliant oratory. And there was Dr Burney, now famous for his *History of Music*, and his 25-year-old daughter Fanny, whose successful novel *Evelina* had whirled her into the midst of the Johnstonian circle as a celebrity when she had finally overcome her ladylike scruples about admitting her authorship. She was Johnson's 'little Fannikin' and she sat at his feet adoring him when he visited the Burneys' home in St Martin's Street or held court at Streatham. But Goldsmith was dead and Garrick died in

1779, followed a year later by Topham Beauclerk. And Mrs Montagu, who had moved herself and her blue-stocking parties to a large new house in Portman Square with a room decorated with hundreds of peacocks' feathers, after quarrelling with Johnson over his criticism of her friend Lord Lyttelton, excluded him from her visiting list. Then in 1781, Henry Thrale died from eating too much beef.

It was the end of an era, the end of Johnson's delectable life of luxury and idleness, surrounded by friends who thought only of his comforts and of pleasing him, and above all of listening while he talked interminably of morals and manners, men and things, with no fear of being contradicted or of not being wanted, only of being teased a little with familiarity and kindness. Hester Thrale mourned for the loss of her husband's income more than for him. She gave up the house at Streatham and then, by the moral standards of the world she belonged to, she did a terrible thing—she fell in love with her daughter's Italian music-master, Gabriele Piozzi. She was forty-one and by no means unattractive. Piozzi was the same age as herself, an accomplished musician with charming manners and a modest background. He was not a fortune-hunter or a cad; he was really very upset and rather embarrassed by the whole business, for the wild, romantic longing in Hester Thrale's breast was all the sharper for having been delayed so long. As a girl she had accepted Thrale to please her dogmatic mother; now, as a woman, she had to face the displeasure of her cold-hearted, eighteen-year-old daughter 'Queeney' and her young sisters. Fanny Burney, rashly acting as the *confidente* of both sides, wrote sententiously to 'Queeney': 'Poor self-deluded Mrs T— How *can* she suffer herself, noble-minded as she is, to be thus duped by ungovernable passions!' And again of her father's reaction to the news: 'He was not at all the less shocked that she should thus fling away her talents,

M

situation in life and character;—for thus to quit all her maternal duties is a blot upon it never to be erased.'

Poor Mrs T—she was indeed much to be pitied, for she was not deluding herself at all. She knew she had to choose between Piozzi and her daughters, who were strongly supported by the conventional attitude of the age with its complex snobbery about everyone's social position and its disapproval of the romantic feeling that now possessed her. She realized that she was inviting the ostracism of society and the censure of her admirers, to say nothing of the hostility she met with from her late husband's trustees. So no wonder she broke out in a rash known as St Anthony's Fire, had hysterics and really thought she would never survive the misery of it all. And no wonder she dared not face Dr Johnson, who, already knowing something of what was going on, wrote tragically: 'Do not, do not drive me from you, for I have not deserved either neglect or hatred.' Once she had called him 'friend, father, guardian, confident—the wisest and best of mortals'; but now she clung to Piozzi with all the romantic intensity of a young girl in her first love-affair, and the day he returned to England was, she wrote, 'the happiest Day of my Life, I think—Yes, *quite* the happiest; my Piozzi came home yesterday and dined with me'.

Johnson, superseded in her affections by a mere musician, a foreigner and a Roman Catholic, reacted ferociously like a wounded bear. 'Madam,' he wrote, 'if I interpret your letter right, you are ignominiously married; if it is yet undone, let us once more talk together. If you have abandoned your children and your religion, God forgive your wickedness; if you have forfeited your fame and your country, may your folly do no further mischief! If the last act is yet to do, I who have loved you, esteemed you, reverenced you and served you, I who long thought you the first of womankind, entreat that, before your fate is irrecoverable, I may once more see you.' But it was no use. Old and sick and miserable, Johnson's life was nearly over and Hester's as the wife of Piozzi only just beginning.

She defended him bravely. 'Oh what a disinterested! what a noble Heart has the man to whom I was this day united!' she exclaimed, and she ignored, or pretended to ignore the malicious gossip going on behind her back. Mrs Montagu, never having known what it was to love anyone except herself, wrote to her blue-stocking friend Mrs Vesey: 'Mrs Thrale's marriage has taken such horrible possession of my mind, I cannot advert to any other subject. I am sorry and feel the worst kind of sorrow, that which is blended with shame . . . I am myself convinced that the poor woman is mad, and indeed have long suspected her mind was disordered. She was the best mother, the best wife, the best friend, the most amiable member of Society . . . I bring in my verdict of lunacy in this affair.' And Mrs Vesey, gloating over the downfall of Mrs T, wrote back that she had heard Piozzi was 'black, ugly and loved nothing but money'. In fact, both ladies were wrong. Hester Piozzi was not insane and her new husband was not in love with her money. They went abroad and settled for a time in Milan, where the Marquis D'Araciel, Piozzi's patron, brought Hester presents, the Abbé Bossi wrote verses in praise of her and the Venetian Envoy, Soderini, 'sent to Venice for *Fish*' for her table. Friends in London held her responsible for Johnson's death a year later and undoubtedly the shock had hastened his decline. But those who believed seriously that she ought to have married him instead of Piozzi, were apparently unaware that this absurd notion was even more romantic and sentimental than her choice of someone her own age, who appealed so strongly to her heart and with whom she lived happily for the next twenty years.

Freedom of choice in matrimony was a new attitude of mind, a revolutionary prospect that inspired the young and scared the old. It caused as much displeasure to parents of the middle classes as to those in the higher reaches of society where it was considered utterly unreasonable for a girl or a boy to marry for love. Thomas Sheridan, that pompous, disappointed and quarrelsome Irish actor, now living in Bath and teaching elocution, oratory and deportment in his Academy for Young Gentlemen, was shocked and horrified by his younger son's attachment to Elizabeth Linley, whose grandfather had been a carpenter, though a prosperous one, and whose father, Thomas Linley, was a musician. Sheridan's Irish clerical family had boasted a bishop or two in the past, which was something he never forgot, and he had little sympathy with Linley's profession, remarking that 'music often draws persons to mix with such company as they would otherwise avoid'. Linley opposed his darling daughter's entanglement with young Dick Sheridan for other reasons—because the boy was penniless, had no settled occupation and never looked like having one, and because his eldest daughter was the brightest jewel in his family.

All the Linley children were talented and exceptionally beautiful. Gainsborough, who took a passionate interest in music and played the violin himself, loved the whole family and painted them over and over again, quite unable to resist their extraordinary fascination. He painted Tom, who played the violin from the age of ten and went to Europe where he made friends with Mozart, who declared that had he lived—he was drowned accidentally at the age of twenty-two—he would have been 'one of the greatest ornaments of the musical world'. He painted Mary, whose voice was almost as lovely as her sister's, and he painted Sam, who played the oboe but gave it up to go to sea, dying of a fever on board ship at the age of eighteen. He painted Eliza with Tom when she was only fourteen, Eliza and Mary together a year or two later, and

Eliza alone, twice if not three times, for he found the
ravishing youthful freshness and the poignant inward
quality of beauty she possessed infinitely more inspiring
than the mere affectation of beauty he saw in so many of
his fashionable sitters.

Eliza was not only exquisite to look at; she had a
sensitive, charming disposition and she sang like an angel.
Her father adored her and had given her his own ardent
love of music besides training her voice with tender care.
But it never occurred to him, or to his rather vulgar and
pedestrian wife, that her success as a concert singer put a
great strain on her delicate physique; nor did they seem to
realize that anyone so attractive was bound to be pestered
by hordes of gentlemen with the worst possible intentions.
What she suffered was appalling. The gossips and the
scandalmongers of Bath and London took her private life
to pieces and turned the bits over in their messy fingers.
The newspapers printed suggestive comments on her
refusal of an elderly suitor residing in Bath, and the odious
Samuel Foote, thinly disguising the whole unhappy affair
for the amusement of the public, dressed it up into a
salacious comedy called *The Maid of Bath,* which was
produced at the Little Theatre in the Haymarket in the
summer of 1771 and set the whole town talking. As if all
this was not enough, the poor girl was also being
molested by a certain 'Captain' Mathews, a rake and a
lady-killer with a wife living in Bath, and she must have
been quite desperate when she confided in Richard Brinsley
Sheridan's young sisters, who promptly rushed to her
rescue by devising a scheme in which they believed their
brother was 'designed by nature to act the part of a knight
of olden time'.

Dick Sheridan—witty, charming, handsome and idle—
found the part exactly to his liking. He bundled the lovely
Eliza into a post-chaise one cold March evening, carried
her off to London and across the Channel through a

frightful storm to Calais, then on to Lille, where an English doctor and his wife took care of the sick and frightened girl. Dick wrote to his brother begging him 'not to be uneasy lest anything should tempt me to depart, even in thought, from the honour and consistency which engaged me at first in this affair'. And he meant it. On his return to England, he sought out Mathews and fought two duels with him, being severely wounded in the second and more serious engagement and lying sick at the White Hart Inn at Bath for eight days. If the elder Sheridan and the elder Linley with their conventional ideas of parental authority thought this was the end of the matter, they were very much mistaken. The flame of romantic love in Eliza's heart naturally burned more fiercely for the young man who had twice offered his life to protect her honour and it was very stupid of Mrs Linley to take her candle and her inkstand away, for she could still write to him by the light of the moon at midnight and in pencil: 'My whole soul is devoted to you, nor would I change my present situation to be wife to any man . . . I feel I love you every day more tenderly.'

By 1773, Eliza had reached the height of her career. 'The applause and admiration she has met with can only be compared to what is given to Mr Garrick,' Fanny Burney wrote after hearing her in London. 'The whole town seems distracted about her. Miss Linley engrosses all eyes, ears and hearts.' And although Fanny was, as usual, rather prim and somewhat critical when she heard that Eliza was 'believed to be very romantic', even she was overcome by 'the beauty of her complexion, her fine, luxurious, easy-sitting hair, charming forehead, pretty mouth and most bewitching eyes', adding that 'with all this her carriage is modest and unassuming and her countenance indicates diffidence and a strong desire of pleasing'. What Fanny missed seeing was the quiet strength of Eliza's character and the depth of her devotion to the man she loved. Nothing could alter this—and when Sheridan came of age, though his wit was still his only income, even Linley at last had sufficient imagination to realize that he could withold his consent to the marriage no longer. Young romantic love had triumphed over middle-aged common sense and reason.

In the same year it triumphed again in the bosom of another girl, one year younger than Eliza. Sarah Kemble, the eldest daughter of Roger Kemble and his wife, born in a public house called the Shoulder of Mutton at Brecon, believed her whole future happiness was dependent on William Siddons, a not very good actor in her father's company of strolling players. Parental opposition forced them apart. William Siddons was dismissed from the troupe with a box on the ear from Mrs Kemble and Sarah sent away to Warwickshire as a companion-maid to Lady Mary Greathead at a salary of £10 a year. Lady Mary, it seems, was rather overcome by the stately appearance of her handsome young maid, for she admitted afterwards that she was always seized with an overwhelming inclination to get up from her chair when she came into the room, but Sarah very quickly adapted herself to a dignified style of domesticity, quite different from the life she had been accustomed to in the theatre. The house was a romantic old stone edifice, described as 'a place of pleasure, mete for the muses . . . with an ancient hermitage . . . a praty wood and the river rolling with a praty voice over the stones'—exactly the kind of setting to stimulate any young girl's lovesick imagination and to make Sarah think of William as the hero of her dreams. She did not waste her time. She studied Milton and was often heard declaiming passages from Shakespeare in the servants' hall—and William came to see her to renew his vows of fidelity, even to suggest an elopement, which she prudently refused, preferring to wear down her parents' resistance. Perhaps the Kembles themselves, like Lady

Mary Greathead, were rather overawed by their daughter's strong personality, or perhaps they came to realize at last that they had bred an eagle not a dove and were frightened of her fiery temper. Whatever the reason they finally consented rather grudgingly and in 1773, at the age of eighteen, Sarah was married to William Siddons at Trinity Church, Coventry.

Marriage was by no means the romantic dream she had visualized. William was no hero at all, and as strolling players they were despised and neglected, travelling up and down the country, acting in wretched theatres or no theatres at all, in barns and public houses, and living from hand to mouth in squalid lodgings. Fortunately Sarah had inherited her mother's ferocious energy and her pride; even so it was a hard life made yet more exacting by the birth of her children and the increasingly obvious inadequacy of her husband. Rumour began to circulate, none the less, that there was a strolling actress of uncommon power in the provinces and Garrick sent off one of his spies to report on her. It was his last year at Drury Lane and he was harassed by his three leading ladies, Mrs Abington, Mrs Yates and Miss Younge, a triumvirate of vanity, envy and jealousy quite beyond his control. To present a new actress to the public, he thought, would perhaps succeed in chastening the malice of the other three; but the new actress lost her nerve: her voice quavered, her tone faltered and died into an inaudible whisper, she looked pale and ill and as Portia, wore an ugly salmon-pink gown as faded as her cheeks—she was an utter failure. Garrick apparently enjoyed the situation. Abington, Yates and Younge tormented him less than they tormented their young rival and although Sarah held her head high, she made no appeal to the public and in no way diminished Garrick's own final blaze of glory. He gave his farewell performance as Richard III in May 1776; Mrs Siddons, according to the only critic who

mentioned her, was 'a lamentable Lady Anne'. She was
not re-engaged by the new management at Drury Lane;
she was driven back to the wearing and sordid existence
of a strolling player in the provinces with a family to
support and no prospect of ever achieving anything
better.

Things were not, however, quite so bad as her highly-
strung, rather morbid temperament induced her to
believe. Compelled by necessity and wounded pride, she
worked harder than ever and having acted with Garrick
in London, was treated with more respect in the best of
the provincial theatres. At Birmingham, Liverpool,
Manchester and York she enhanced her reputation in both
comedy and tragedy, attracting friends wherever she went
by the magnetism, the smouldering fire and the dignity
of her bearing. Then in 1778 she accepted an offer from
John Palmer to act at the Theatre Royal in Bath before the
most critical and sophisticated audience outside London,
an audience all too easily bored by the surfeit of leisure
and pleasure they enjoyed in the spacious, tea-drinking,
gossip-ridden city. The Linleys and the Sheridans had
moved to London—old Thomas Sheridan only came back
occasionally to drink the waters for his gout. The people
of Bath wanted a new sensation, something that would stir
their emotions and heighten their tired sensibility; and
that was precisely what Sarah Siddons gave them when
she appeared as Elwina in Hannah More's turgid tragedy,
Percy. The indescribable pathos of her acting swept them
off their feet. They wept and went mad—as London was
to go mad four years later when she returned in triumph
to Drury Lane and was hailed by the public and the critics
alike as 'beyond all comparison the first tragic actress now
on the English stage'.

It had taken Sarah Siddons more than ten years to
establish herself and to create a style of her own which
appealed to the new instinct of the public for emotional

expression. She claimed that her art was derived directly from nature and so it seemed to her infatuated audience. Women had hysterics when she played the innocent and tragic Jane Shore, gentlemen sobbed and 'fainting fits were long and frequent in the house'. The theatre was besieged. King George and Queen Charlotte with the Prince of Wales and his two eldest sisters watched her from a box draped in crimson velvet and white satin. She was mobbed in the streets, invited hither and thither by fashionable society, painted by Gainsborough, Reynolds and a dozen or so lesser artists, and accused not only of making a fortune, but of sitting on it. In fact, her astonishing success brought her little personal pleasure and even less as the years went on, for she was most cruelly persecuted by her enemies in the theatrical profession, worn out by constantly working much too hard to support her large family and irritated beyond measure by the husband she had once looked upon as a romantic hero. He was jealous of the furore she created, mean with her money, stupid about his children and sadly aware, as he once said of his wife, that 'she is too grand a thing for me'.

Yet the splendour and the passion of her acting continued to hypnotize her audience, and it was not only the affluent folk of the town who were obsessed by 'her succession of astonishing changes in the interpretation of grief and anguish', but young men of modest means and intellectual discrimination, proudly exercising their newly discovered critical faculties on the pleasures of life and art. Thomas Lawrence, precocious as a boy in Bristol and at seventeen convinced that he could risk his reputation 'for the painting of a head' with any other artist in London except Sir Joshua, sat at her feet, endlessly drawing and painting her expressive features, before he became an intimate friend of her family and created havoc in it by transferring his affections from one of her daughters to the other, making 'violent scenes of the most painful emotion' in the process, 'in a paroxysm of self-abandoned misery' equal to anything that Mrs Siddons herself had ever demonstrated on the stage. William Hazlitt, a boy of sixteen studying at Hackney College to become a Unitarian Minister, a prospect he viewed with the utmost misgivings, fought through the mob of gallery-ites for standing room at Drury Lane and years later was to write: 'She was not less than a goddess or a prophetess inspired by the gods. Power was seated on her brow, passion emanated from her breast like a shrine. . . . She not only hushed the tumultuous shouts of the pits in breathless expectation, and quenched the blaze of surrounding beauty in silent tears, but to the retired and lonely student, through long years of solitude, her face has shone as if an eye had appeared from heaven, her name has been as if a voice had opened the chambers of the human heart, or as if a trumpet had awakened the sleeping and the dead.'

Hazlitt never forgot. She fired his youthful imagination and 'filled his cup of pleasure to the full'. She released in him all the pent-up emotion of a soul longing to break free from the restrictions imposed by a Nonconformist upbringing. When he beheld Mrs Siddons's blazing eyes and heard her resounding voice, the potential artist and writer in him was stirred to rebel against the spiritual incompetence of the Unitarian creed; here was a sublime revelation, unsuspected by the denizens of Hackney College, a voice bidding him to express the chaotic inner thoughts and feelings that so disturbed him and to seek for eternal truth. No other inspiration was quite so profound or quite so intoxicating, except his meeting four years later with Samuel Taylor Coleridge, who came to Shrewsbury to preach in the Unitarian chapel there and was entertained by Hazlitt's father at Wem.

He arrived 'talking at a great rate'—and did not cease

talking while he stayed. 'A sound was in my ears as of a siren's song,' Hazlitt wrote. 'I was stunned, startled with it, as from deep sleep, . . .The light of his genius shone into my soul, like the sun's glittering in the puddles of the road.' Here was a preacher with a difference, and as with Mrs Siddons, someone who spoke directly from the heart, uniting poetry and philosophy with a spirit of hope that turned everything in nature to good. Enthusiasm glowed 'in the darkened lustre of his eyes', as he poured forth an eloquent stream of ideas, opinions and mystical observations, 'passing from one subject to another as if floating in the air'. Hazlitt was dizzy with excitement, overcome with delight when Coleridge invited him to Nether Stowey and filled with exultation at the thought of seeing him again. 'In the meantime,' he wrote, 'I went to Llangollen Vale by way of initiating myself in the mysteries of natural scenery; and I must say I was enchanted with it. I had been reading Coleridge's description of England in his fine *Ode on the Departing Year*, and I applied it, *con amore,* to the objects before me. That valley was to me the cradle of a new existence: in the river that winds through it, my spirit was baptized in the waters of Helicon.'

He was not disappointed when he finally arrived at Nether Stowey and became more intimate with Coleridge, for this highly imaginative, introspective and enthralling young man who never stopped talking and was still in his early twenties, had the most remarkable effect on everyone with whom he came into contact. At Cambridge, during the period of the French Revolution, he had been an ardent Republican; then he became engrossed in Pantisocracy, the high-sounding title he gave to his own scheme for the reformation of the human race. Only kindred souls, Robert Southey among them, were to be admitted to this utopian society, which Coleridge fervently believed could be set up in the backwoods of America—that is, until he endeavoured to put his mind to the practical ways and means of making his idealism work, whereupon the whole dream of a better world collapsed and he sought refuge instead in marrying Southey's sister-in-law, Sara Fricker, who loved him but failed from the very beginning to understand his maddening, mercurial changes of mood and the airy, fantastic flights of his genius.

His friends knew better—to them he was irresistible and a constant inspiration. Charles Lamb, his former schoolfellow at Christ's Hospital, worshipped him. Joseph Cottle, a bookseller in Bristol, published his first volume of poems and helped him with money. Josiah Wedgwood gave him an annuity, so that he would have time enough to devote himself to poetry instead of preaching. Thomas Poole, a farmer at Nether Stowey with a great deal of practical ability, fell completely under his spell and promised he would stand by him 'in sickness or in health, in prosperity or misfortune'. William and Dorothy Wordsworth loved him on sight. Of his first visit to them at Racedown, they recalled how 'he did not keep to the high road, but leapt over a gate and bounded down the pathless field' towards them; and Dorothy wrote to her friend Mary Hutchinson: 'He is a wonderful man. His conversation teems with soul, mind and spirit. . . . At first I thought him very plain, that is, for about three minutes; he is pale and thin, has a wide mouth, thick lips, and not very good teeth, longish, loose-growing, half-curling, rough black hair. But if you hear him speak for five minutes you think no more of this. His eye . . . speaks every emotion of his animated mind; it has more of "the poet's eye in a fine frenzy rolling" than I ever witnessed.'

It was not long since Dorothy Wordsworth had achieved her one and only ambition—that of devoting her whole life to her beloved brother William. Even as children together their sympathy was instinctive and when separated from each other after their mother's death,

Dorothy never ceased to cling to the idea of being reunited with him, though this was against the wishes of
all her guardians and relations, who were highly displeased with William's irresponsible behaviour. Moody at
Cambridge, mad with enthusiasm for the French Revolution and worse, entangled on his first visit to the Continent
with a Frenchwoman who bore him a child, it was not to
be wondered at if they had little faith in his future. He
hated London, refused to go into the church and did not
fancy studying law. He only wanted a quiet life in the
country, to meditate and brood over nature in the hope of
discovering its message to mankind; and it was only
Dorothy, sensitive, loving and single-minded in her
purpose, who understood his need. A timely legacy of
£900 from his friend Raisley Calvert, the promise of a
small, furnished house in Dorset and the proposal that he
and Dorothy should take charge of another friend's small
boy, suddenly changed the whole pattern of their lives,
bringing them together at last and for ever.

Dorothy's joy was overwhelming. 'I think Racedown
is the place dearest to my recollections upon the whole
surface of the island,' she wrote later. 'It is the first home
I had.' The house had 'the prettiest little parlour that can
be' and there were many pleasant walks round about, the
distant hills reminding them both of their native wilds in
Cumberland. They walked for miles and for hours at a
time to the top of Blackdown Hill and Lewesdon Hill,
listening to the birds, looking at the trees, watching the
ever-changing sky and the cloud shadows racing each
other over the hills and the sea. Dorothy had 'an exquisite
regard for common things—she welcomed what was given
and craved no more'; and her delight quickened her
brother's response to their surroundings, healed his
disillusionment with the bloody horrors of the French
Revolution and his feelings of guilt towards the mother of
his child. Dorothy was his inspiration:

> She gave me eyes, she gave me ears,
> And humble cares, and delicate fears;
> A heart the fountain of sweet tears;
> And love, and thought, and joy.

Their isolation was their joy, but when Coleridge leapt across the gate into their lives, their felicity was even greater. He seemed the perfect companion to their vivid pleasure in each other: intellectual, imaginative, tireless, and eager to share their simple way of life. It was not long before he came to their door with a one-horse chaise and carried them off 'over forty miles of execrable roads' to stay with him at Nether Stowey. Mrs Coleridge upset a skillet of boiling milk over his foot, but welcomed his friends quite kindly; and here, at Alfoxden, within walking distance of Coleridge's cottage, they found another home for themselves at a rent they could afford. Hardly a day passed when they had settled at Alfoxden without Coleridge coming over to see them. Brother and sister and their friend were 'three persons and one soul'. They tramped for miles across the hills, 'loitering long and pleasantly in the combes', aware of their delight in each other, of the glorious green turf under their feet and the wide sky above them, for as yet there was no cloud on their horizon.

If Sarah Coleridge was sometimes rather plaintive and Coleridge himself suddenly dejected, he could always be sure of his friends' sympathy. He and Wordsworth were collaborating in a new volume of poems to be called *Lyrical Ballads* and there was no reason to suppose in 1798 that this would not be the forerunner of a still greater harvest in the future. Yet with the dawn of the new century when the Wordsworths moved to Grasmere and Coleridge followed them there, he was already a sick man, experimenting on his own body with the most dangerous of all remedies. 'The poet is dead in me,' he wrote. 'My imagination lies like cold snuff on the circular rim of a brass candlestick, without even a stink of tallow to remind you that it was once clothed and mitred with flame.' *Kubla Khan* lay unfinished; the 'stately pleasure-dome' of the poet's vision had dissolved and vanished in a thickening and disastrous haze of opium.

10

THE GIDDY WORLD

WORDSWORTH'S DISLIKE OF London was not surprising. With his passion for nature, his distaste for crowds and for the confusion of a great city congested with humanity, there was nothing London could offer him, except as seen from Westminster Bridge in the calm of the early morning, 'all bright and glittering in the smokeless air'. Then it was beautiful in his sight, as it had been to Canaletto when he first came to England in 1746 under the patronage of the Duke of Richmond and as it was to the English artists, Samuel Scott and William Marlow, painting somewhat in the style of the Venetian master.

The marvellous spires of Wren's churches and the great dome of St Paul's dominated the skyline, if on a closer view, the city itself was still a rabbit-warren of narrow courts and dark alleys swarming with craftsmen and their apprentices, booksellers, jewellers and all manner of tradesmen working cheek by jowl with the successful

bankers, stock-jobbers, merchants and nabobs of the East
India Company. The river, though of less importance as a
highway than in the beginning of the century, was
crowded with ocean-going ships from the farthest corners
of the world in the tidal waters of the port and with
pleasure-boats sailing upstream to Vauxhall Gardens,
Chelsea and the sweet suburbs of Hampton Court,
Richmond and Twickenham. The rebuilding of Somerset
House in 1776 to house the Royal Academy and other
learned institutions, the covering over of the nauseous
Fleet Ditch and the airy riverside frontage of Adelphi
Terrace designed by the Adam brothers as a speculative
proposition, were all Georgian improvements worthy of
the golden age of taste. Westminster Bridge, the first new
bridge to be built over the Thames for 500 years, and
Blackfriars Bridge built ten years later in 1760, excited the
admiration of everyone and brought Londoners out in the
evening to stroll backwards and forwards across the river
as the sun was setting; while in Westminster itself, well-
proportioned streets and squares of houses were built
over the pig farms and the sodden marshes of Tothill
Fields.

In Bloomsbury, the Dukes of Bedford had been steadily
developing their property ever since the beginning of the
century, and in the fields of Marylebone between Oxford
Street (as the Oxford Road was called after 1783) and the
New Road from Paddingon to Islington, the Portman and
Cavendish-Harley estates were laid out with dignity,
sobriety and elegance. 'The new squares in the West End
are carefully planned and pleasing to the eye,' one
foreigner wrote, 'and the upper classes who live there find
them salubrious, since within each of them is a magnificent
garden and the surrounding houses are tall with plenty of
big windows.' Even sanitation was improving. Adam
included a water-closet in his plans for Lord Derby's
house in Grosvenor Square, conveniently situated next to

his lordship's dressing-room instead of out in the garden
by the stables, and this was served by a brick drain connected with the public sewer. 'Bath houses' were rare
enough to be thought eccentric, but water was laid on by
the New River Company or the Chelsea Waterworks for a
small quarterly rate and stored in decorative lead cisterns.

Yet with all this building going on everywhere, there
were still plenty of open spaces where Londoners of all
classes were able to enjoy their leisure in countrified surroundings. If they got tired of the royal parks and the
pleasure gardens, they could walk or drive to the taverns
and tea gardens in the villages of Knightsbridge, Kilburn
and Islington, drink fresh milk from the cows at Chalk
Farm and eat strawberries picked in the market gardens
of Lambeth and Brompton. And in 1784 they poured into
the Artillery Ground at Moorfields to watch Vincent
Lunardi, the handsome young secretary to the Neapolitan
Ambassador, launch himself into the skies in his air
balloon, with a cat and a pigeon to keep him company
and a bottle of wine and a leg of cold chicken to appease
his hunger. He kindly came down at North Mimms to put
the cat out because it was suffering from the cold, ascend-
ing again to continue his delectable flight to a village near
Ware in Hertfordshire, where he landed safely, to be fêted
on his return to London as a hero.

Horace Walpole did not approve of all the excitement.
'He had full right to venture his own neck,' he wrote,
'but none to risk the poor cat,' and he was disappointed
because the 'airgonaut' had not got anywhere near the
moon. He foretold—wrongly—that 'Balloonism' would
soon explode and make everyone look extremely foolish,
when, in fact, it caught the imagination of the public and
sent them racing off again to St George's Fields in
Newington Butts to see the even more daring ascent of
the 'First English Female Aerial Traveller', a certain Mrs
Sage, who was buxom as well as brave and stepped into

the car of Lunardi's balloon wearing a huge velvet hat trimmed with ostrich-feathers. She was accompanied by George Biggin, a friend of Lunardi's, who brought her down in a field not far from Harrow School, where the boys ran out to meet her, waving their hats and cheering as they crowded round her to applaud her triumph.

Foreigners visiting London were astonished by the good nature of the crowds that gathered on the slightest pretext to mob their favourite heroes, and sometimes they mistook the ordinary bustle of the streets for some great occasion, scarcely believing it was possible for so much traffic and for so many people to be out and about on their daily business. In the more elegant quarters of the city they were particularly impressed by the clean new paving raised above the muddy level of the streets for the benefit of the pedestrians, and by the street lighting. Sophie von la Roche, the wife of a counsellor in Coblenz, was fascinated by the brilliance of the streets at night. Public lighting was reinforced by the innumerable lamps displayed by the shops to emphasize the beauty of their window-displays. Apothecaries used giant, coloured glass jars filled with liquid as reflectors; jewellers, clock-makers, silk-mercers and fan-makers set their goods off by the glitter of different lanterns cleverly disposed among them; sweet shops and fruit stalls, piled high with grapes and figs and expensive pineapples, were lit by hanging lamps of all shapes and sizes. No wonder Oxford Street, which by now had quite surpassed the Strand for quality and variety in its shops, had 'as many people in it as there were in all Frankfurt, when the Fair was on', according to Sophie, and that they stayed there until late at night, the idle window-gazers being joined by the fashionable audience leaving the near-by Pantheon, Wyatt's stately new concert hall built in 1772 at a cost of £90,000 and considered to be 'the most elegant structure in Europe, if not on the globe'.

Sophie went there, of course—she went everywhere, returning again and again to the shops, which she found irresistible and far superior to anything she had seen in Paris or anywhere else. The pastrycooks made her mouth water, 'with all kinds of preserved fruits and jellies exhibited in handsome glass jars, pyramids of small pastries and tartlets and sweetmeats, all attractively set out under a delightful gauze covering which hid nothing and at the same time kept the flies off'. Even the butchers' shops were 'deliciously clean, with all the goods spread on snow-white cloths, and cloths of a similar whiteness stretched out behind the large hunks of meat hanging up: no blood anywhere and no dirt'. And she admired the shop assistants for being courteous but for 'not cringing to people of rank and affluence'. She was, in fact, enraptured by everything she saw in London. She had arrived with a predisposition to like the English and she was not disappointed. She saw the more equal distribution of the good things of life in 'England and the comparative lack of class distinction amongst London's inhabitants . . . as far more pleasing to the philanthropist's heart than the sight of a hundred palaces, the property of might and wealth, jammed up against thousands of miserable hovels' as in Paris or in Germany. She rejoiced in the sylvan beauty of St James's Park and the Green Park, where 'all good people who cannot afford country seats and who wear their eyes out at their daily toil . . . could rest their eyes in the evening on the verdant green and refresh themselves in the air'. She did not go anywhere near the rookery of St Giles or into the stews of Covent Garden and Clare Market, still seething with immorality and vice; but when she came out of the Little Theatre in the Haymarket in a downpour and could not find a sedan-chair, she did ruin her black hat 'with the embroidered crape' because she realized that it was safer to walk home than 'to loiter outside the theatre with the crowd of light women', though even then she thought they were all better dressed than she was and looked 'extremely pretty'.

Evidently Sophie only saw what she wanted to see and never took her rose-coloured spectacles off. But she enjoyed herself immensely. She did all the things a tourist was expected to do and a lot more besides. She visited Westminster Abbey, admired the weeping Britannia on Lord Chatham's colossal new tomb and was surprised by the wax effigy of the Duchess of Richmond in her crumbling court-dress of green velvet with her stuffed dog and parrot by her side. She went to Montagu House to see the treasures of the British Museum, founded in 1759, and met a number of her fellow Germans there, poring over the Etruscan and Roman antiquities collected by Sir William Hamilton. She saw the all-black tiger brought home from the East Indies by Warren Hastings in its cage at the Tower and was shocked by the way the crown jewels and the regalia were kept in 'an old smoky cupboard' in one of the vaults, dimly lit by two tallow candles and shown to the visitors by an ancient harridan of 'the most ungainly appearance'.

Warren Hastings and his German wife were among her friends and so was the astronomer William Herschel, who had given up music for the stars and sat her in the chair of his telescope in his garden at Slough, winding her up in it so that she 'beheld the Heavens with rapture'. Then at Windsor, she met Mrs Delany, now nearly ninety years old, and Fanny Burney, with whom she had 'an extremely pleasant discussion', admiring 'her personal grace, her mental accomplishments and her modesty' and believing that 'all noble-minded, rational beings would delight in her acquaintance and feel at home with her'. Fanny, writing in her diary of the same meeting which she had done her best to avoid, was much less enthusiastic. 'She [Sophie] is now *bien passée*,' she remarked, 'no doubt fifty—yet has a voice of touching sweetness, eyes of dove-

like gentleness, looks supplicating for favour and an air
the most tenderly caressing. . . . Had I met her in any other
way she might have pleased me in no common degree.'
As it was, Fanny was so miserable at Windsor as a Woman
of the Bedchamber to the Queen with no freedom from
'the tyranny, exigeance and ennui' of the Court and so cut
off from her family and her friends, she found Sophie's
sentimental gush more than she could bear.

The crown of Sophie's visit was her audience with the
royal family at the Castle. She rhapsodized over 'the generous condescension . . . the beautiful eyes, beautiful
expression and gracious countenance' of the dumpy little
German Queen, whose appearance even Gainsborough
could not make attractive. She thought the King 'a most
distinguished and handsome man' and when 'he laid his
hand upon his breast with fine, manly frankness' and told
her he could never forget that his heart pulsed with
German blood, she nearly swooned with delight. She had
no idea that his courtiers found him dull and stupid,
obstinate, cunning and totally lacking in social grace even
before he was seized with fits of insanity, or that their
attendance on him was a painful duty, not a pleasure. For
King George III, of whom so much had been hoped in
1760, had proved to be as unsatisfactory in many ways as
his grandfather, King George II, and more unmanageable
politically. According to Horace Walpole, 'he lost his
dominions in America, his authority over Ireland and all
influence in Europe by aiming at despotism in England'.
He was condescending and kind enough to the farmers
round about Windsor, showing a keen interest in their
cattle and their crops. He was enthusiastic about Handel's
music and Benjamin West's enormous historical paintings,
and in his private life, very abstemious, preferring to dine
alone off a leg of mutton with caper sauce and to mix his
wine with water. But he bullied his ministers and his Queen
with an implacable air of authority and detested his eldest

son, who retaliated by showing his father no filial respect whatever.

Indeed, the Prince of Wales grew up in the pattern of discontent that had dogged the House of Hanover from the time of George I: the father hating the son and the son breaking away from parental control to set up a rival Court, which soon became the focus of the Opposition in Parliament and of everyone else with a grievance against the King. And the Prince was not entirely to blame if he showed a disposition for enjoying himself at the expense of his family. Too much Teutonic discipline in his youth had bred resentment and a desire for independence, a greedy curiosity to taste the pleasures of life and a persistent need to display his own talents, for so long frustrated by his father's jealous surveillance. He was besides an extremely handsome young man, with a high colour, vivid blue eyes and a good figure, his shapely legs clad in immaculate stockings and his embroidered silk coat and skin-tight breeches a costly advertisement for his tailor. He had an easy, distinguished air about him that charmed everyone—not only his intimate friends like the wildly extravagant Barrymore brothers, Fox, Sheridan and the Duchess of Devonshire, but the populace also, who thought the country was fortunate in having an heir to the throne so unlike his uncouth brothers and his red-faced uncle the Duke of Cumberland.

It was, however, his uncle Cumberland who, being on very bad terms with the King, led him into his first dissipations, so that before he came of age and was still living in Buckingham House, he had learnt to gamble and to pursue his own pleasure with zest and self-indulgence. He no sooner saw Mrs Robinson, the twenty-year-old actress with 'a divine face and figure' playing Perdita in *A Winter's Tale* than he fixed his attention upon her, sending his equerry Lord Maldon round to her house the next morning with a *billet-doux* signed Florizel; and

although Perdita, who had suffered most cruelly from her
husband's vicious conduct, pretended for quite a time not
to know what Florizel had in mind, he made so many
eloquent assurances of his undying affection for her and
got himself into such a state of agitation that she finally
agreed to a secret meeting in the gardens of the Queen's
palace at Kew, being conveyed there in a rowing-boat in
the dusk of the evening. 'A few words, and those scarcely
articulated, uttered by the Prince . . . the graces of his
person, the irresistible sweetness of his smile and the
tenderness of his melodious yet manly voice' conquered
her reluctance altogether and a bond promising her the
sum of £20,000 to be paid when he came of age seemed to
confirm his generosity. Alas, poor Perdita—the rapturous
delight she gave the Prince did not last. Three years later
she might have been seen travelling alone across Houns-
low Heath in her pony-phaeton with only the protection
of a nine-year-old postilion, on her way to Windsor,
where her royal lover refused to see her or to give her any
explanation of his sudden coldness towards her. His
promise of £20,000 was not redeemed either, though
Fox eventually persuaded him to give her an annuity of
£500 a year and is said to have enjoyed her 'friendship' in
consequence.

Charles James Fox—himself a compulsive gambler, a
brilliant wit and a delightful companion—had some
influence over the Prince and was more deeply involved
in his next and far more serious amorous adventure. For
in 1784, soon after the Prince had moved to Carlton
House, he fell madly in love with Mrs Fitzherbert. She was
plump and pretty, with fair gold hair and a pink and white
complexion: twice a widow, though still in her twenties,
and a Roman Catholic. She would not be his mistress and
could not be his legal wife under the Royal Marriages
Act of Parliament. But the Prince staged a dramatic
attempt at suicide and the poor lady, summoned in haste

by his surgeon and the Duchess of Devonshire, found him 'very pale and covered in blood'. What could she do? She loved him and he swore that he could not live without her, 'using the most extravagant expressions . . . rolling on the floor, striking his forehead, tearing his hair and falling into hysterics'. Nothing would pacify him or induce him to give her up. When she withdrew to France for a while, he sent every courier of the realm after her with his frenzied letters, until the French Government became suspicious, believing some political plot was afoot, and Mrs Fitzherbert had no option but to return quietly to England, where at last the Prince persuaded her—no one quite knew how—to marry him secretly in her own drawing-room.

The marriage was conducted by a curate belonging to the Church of England and it seemed to satisfy Mrs Fitzherbert's delicate conscience. It gave the emotional Prince what he wanted and since it was assumed that Mrs Fitzherbert had consented to become his mistress, the younger set in the fast and giddy world of high society accepted them both. Rumours of the marriage, however, began to circulate and it was Fox who categorically denied that any such marriage had taken place when the Prince's debts came up for consideration in the House of Commons fifteen months later. He genuinely believed that he was speaking the truth, only to be told some hours later by a member of Brooks's Club that he was mistaken, by which time there was nothing he could do except keep his mouth shut and let Sheridan cover up the whole affair in the next debate in Parliament.

Dick Sheridan had come a very long way since his romantic marriage to Elizabeth Linley. He had written two of the best comedies in the English language, *The Rivals* and *The School for Scandal,* was the owner on borrowed money of Drury Lane, a Member of Parliament through the influence of the young Duchess of Devon-

shire and by this time a gentleman of considerable power
and importance, trying very hard to forget that he had ever
been the son of an actor. At the very beginning of his
married life he had forbidden his wife to sing any more in
public, though not at their own musical parties, which
thus became a magnet for the rich and distinguished
members of the beau-monde whose society he wished to
cultivate. Eliza Sheridan, adoring him—he was still so
gay and attractive—acquiesced; and without giving
herself a moment's leisure, contributed far more to his
success than he ever really realized. She handled the
complicated financial affairs of Drury Lane, which he was
only too anxious to forget so long as he was provided with
ready money, helped her father in arranging and composing the music for the theatre, copied Sheridan's
confidential political papers and with her exquisite
grace and intelligence, shone among his fashionable
friends.

'Her life would kill a horse,' Sheridan's sister Betsy
wrote—and it did kill her before she was forty; 'but
amusement she says is the way to banish disagreeable
reflections', a statement which was some way from the
truth. For Eliza went to the opera and the theatre, to balls,
routs and masquerades that went on into the early hours
of the morning, mainly to give her husband pleasure by
keeping up with his worldly aspirations and sometimes to
disguise her own unhappiness at his devotion to the
wealthy Mrs Crewe of Crewe Hall and to the young
Duchess of Devonshire's sister, Lady Duncannon.
'Believe me, my dear Dick,' she once wrote to him when
things were not going very well, 'you *have* a resource if
you really love *me* better than your ambition. Take me
out of the whirl of the world, place me in the quiet and
simple scenes of life I was born for, and you will see
that I shall once more be in my element, and if I saw you
content, I should be happy.' But it was no use. Her dear

Dick was more fond of his ambition and he never saw that he was wearing her out until it was too late.

Betsy, though she had a great affection for her brother and sister-in-law, found it difficult to keep up with their way of life in Bruton Street. During the Regency crisis of 1788 when the King was raving at Windsor, there was a constant coming and going at all hours of the day and night, the Prince himself arriving unannounced to consult with Sheridan, or coming to supper with Mrs Fitzherbert, the Duke of York, Fox, the Duchess of Devonshire, Lord Townshend and a crowd of his supporters. Betsy liked the good humour and simplicity of Fox, but crept away upstairs as soon as she could and steadily refused invitations to the balls and assemblies at Devonshire House. She did, however, consent—'with as little pleasure as ever I did anything in my life'—to go to the masquerade at Mrs Stuart's house in Hammersmith, disguised as a gipsy in a dress she thought 'very ugly'; and when she got there she was quite overcome by the splendour of the pillared hall paved with marble. The ball room was decorated with 'colour'd lamps ornamented with a transparency representing the Prince's crest . . . and with Natural flowers in abundance' and the dancing started at ten o'clock, though the Prince and Mrs Fitzherbert, 'in a White dress and black veil but unlike a Nun's dress', did not arrive until one o'clock and supper did not begin before two. The Prince put Mrs Sheridan on his right and the Duchess of Ancaster 'as *Hecate*' on his left, and Betsy sat next to her brother with Lady Duncannon opposite 'as a *Soeur Grise*, casting many tender looks across the table'. After supper when some of the gentlemen were rather far gone with wine, some excellent catch-singers entertained the company and the Prince asked Mrs Sheridan to join him in a duet, which she did at once, though taken quite by surprise. 'He has a good voice and being so well supported seem'd to me to sing very well,' Betsy remarked,

but this 'peep at the Raree Show of the great world' did
not seduce her into liking it; with the puritanism of the
middle classes, she looked askance at the goings-on in high
society and longed for 'the real comfort and happyness' she
hoped to enjoy with her future husband, Henry Le Fanu.

She disapproved of the glamorous young Duchess of
Devonshire. 'She cannot I think be call'd fat,' she wrote,
'but upon the whole I think there is too much of her. She
gives me the idea of being *larger* than life. I do not think
her Ellegant. She was here [in Bruton Street] last night
and with her Lady Elizabeth Forster who lives with her
and is her bosom friend, but is supposed to be more
particularly the friend of the Duke—such is the system of
the fine World. As to the Dutchess, tho' we Who stand at
awfull distance consider her character in a respectable light
I find among her *friends* She is by no means supposed to
be sparing of her *smiles* at least.' Betsy's rather caustic
judgement was hardly fair on the Duchess, who had been
exposed to the temptations of the world from a very early
age and could not really be blamed if she showed some
lack of discretion. Even her ambitious mother, Lady
Spencer, had not been without misgivings about marrying
her off on her seventeenth birthday to the most eligible
duke in England. 'Georgiana is indeed a lovely young
woman, very pleasing in her figure, but infinitely more so
from her character and disposition,' she wrote to a friend
of hers. 'My dread is that she will be snatched from me
before her age and experience make her fit for the serious
duties of a wife, a mother or the mistress of a family. . . .
She is amiable, innocent and benevolent, but she is giddy,
idle and fond of dissipation. . . . I should have had more
time to improve her understanding . . . and enabled her to
avoid the many snares that vice and folly will throw in her
way.'

Yet the marriage was happy and successful in the beginning. If not a great beauty in the classical sense, Georgiana

had everything else: style and gaiety, dazzling charm and a warm-hearted, impetuous disposition which constantly led her into what she ingenuously described as one 'scrape' after another. With her fascination, her youth and her spontaneity, she immediately became the focus of the younger generation in society and a leader of fashion. Everyone copied her simple muslin dresses sashed at the waist and frilled at the bosom, the tall plumes she wore with the diamonds in her hair and the devastating tilt of her hats. Devonshire House and Chatsworth had not had a mistress since the death of the last Duchess twenty years before and now suddenly, the darkened rooms blazed with light, the chandeliers glittered and the mirrors reflected the kaleidoscopic patterns of the rich, the idle and the gay as they danced to the sound of the musicians in the gallery. The Duke, whose chief characteristic according to one of his friends, was apathy, remained somewhat aloof; the Duchess attracted everyone and, as time went on, the fury of the press also—one writer accusing her of 'succumbing entirely to the seductions of Pleasure and of yielding to the Delusions which played around her'. In fact, she was quite aware of her own reckless way of running wild when her heart ruled her head, as in the Prince's affair with Mrs Fitzherbert, or in the Westminster Election of 1784 when she gained an appalling notoriety by canvassing for Fox because she believed in him and loved him. She tried to explain it all to her anxious mother. 'Dst Mama, I repent, as I often do, the part I have taken, tho' I don't see how I cd have done otherways,' she wrote, though this admission failed to mollify Lady Spencer, who was horribly vexed by the disgusting cartoons appearing in the newspapers and feared for her beloved daughter's reputation.

She worried incessantly about Georgiana—and especially about her equivocal relationship with the Duke's pretty little *chère amie*, Lady Elizabeth Foster. To Lady

Spencer, belonging to an older generation not necessarily
more moral than her daughter's, but ready to believe that
the young in pursuing their pleasure were going quite
beyond the limits of decency and decorum, the situation
was deplorable and all the more so for being the talk of the
town. No one was deceived by Lady Elizabeth's hasty
withdrawal to the Continent on two occasions, or by the
children who afterwards appeared in the Devonshire
House schoolroom to be brought up with Georgiana's
own; everyone noticed the Duke's indifference to his
Duchess and his more animated expression when in the
company of Lady Elizabeth. Yet the Duchess professed
to adore her and seemingly did so. Perhaps she found the
Duke easier to manage when his mistress was in the house,
or perhaps she had given up trying to look for a response
from his strangely reserved, lethargic disposition. Whatever the reason she truly idolized Lady Elizabeth and was
very angry when her mother tried to interfere. 'You are
wrong, grossly wrong, Dst Mama,' she wrote. 'I have the
highest regard and respect and esteem for Ly Eliz. as well
as love. In this case, Dst M., you must feel how impossible, how cruel it would be to expose her to the
malignant ill-nature of the world and to expose ourselves
to all the misery of parting with her for what we know to
be unjust and false.' So Lady Elizabeth, 'dearest Bess' to
both of them, stayed curled up on the carpet at Devonshire House like a pussy-cat warming itself by the fire and
Lady Spencer had to grieve in silence.

    She grieved even more about her daughter's increasing
debts, due to her shocking extravagance and to her mania
for gambling. 'Play at whist, commerce, backgammon,
trictrac or chess,' Lady Spencer wrote, 'but never at
quinze, lou, brag, faro, hazard or any games of chance'—
advice that surely should have been given sooner, since
Georgiana remembered 'playing from 7 in the morning
till 8 at night at Lansquenet with old Mrs Newton when I

was nine years old and was sent to the King's Road for the measles' and not unnaturally concluded that her addiction was by now incurable. As the Duke invariably played faro when at home in the evenings and all his friends had a similar lust for gambling, it was hardly possible for his Duchess to heed her mother's warning and 'make the fashionable excuse of being tied up not to play such and such a game'. She often tried and always failed, was often rescued by her mother paying her losses without the Duke's knowledge but, as she got more involved, she frequently 'forgot' one or two debts of six or seven thousand pounds, or failed to tell the truth, if she really knew it, about the astronomical sums involved. She appealed privately to Thomas Coutts, the banker, to extricate her from her difficulties, and he admonished her like a father. 'I should be happy beyond expression if I could think I have even the smallest share in saving your Grace from the dreadful consequences I foresee,' he wrote. But it was hopeless. By the time she was thirty she owed more than £60,000 and though outwardly her life was still a dazzling round of extravagant entertainment, inwardly it was vexed by the appalling entanglement she had got herself into and a growing awareness of the disaster which lay ahead.

Deep play had affected the aristocracy all through the century, but now had more of a hold than ever over the young, whose pride and extravagance were seldom tempered by the Palladian ideal of restraint advocated in the past by Pope and Lord Burlington. The sober, moralizing influence of Dr Johnson and his friends had also gone out of fashion; the artists and the intellectuals were absorbed in nature and the new romanticism and found London less to their liking than the country. The coffee houses and the chocolate houses, where the writers and the nobility had once forgathered on equal terms, had declined in favour of the new and more exclusive clubs

founded in the 1760s and the 1770s in St James's Street.
Here, at White's, Boodle's and Brooks's palatial new
premises, members settled down to gamble through the
night. 'They began by pulling off their embroidered
coats, put on frieze great-coats, or turned their coats
inside outwards for luck. They put on pieces of leather,
such as worn by footmen when they clean knives, to save
their lace ruffles; and to guard their eyes from the light,
and to prevent tumbling their hair, wore high-crowned
straw hats with broad brims adorned with flowers and
ribbons, and masks to conceal their emotions when they
played at Quinze.' Not to show any emotion, even when
utterly ruined, was all part of the game. Fox, on one
occasion when his last guinea had gone, was found
calmly reading a book.

From the age of sixteen onwards, he was in the habit of
sitting at cards from ten o'clock in the evening until six
the following morning and by the time he was twenty-five,
his debts amounted to close on £250,000. He called his
ante-room, 'the Jerusalem Chamber' from the number of
Jewish money-lenders he entertained there, who provided
him with enough cash to return to the tables and try his
luck once more. Yet his ability as a statesman and his
powers as the spokesman of the Whig Opposition in
Parliament were seldom impaired by lack of sleep or the
prospect of ruin, and his friends all adored him. His eyes
were described by the Swiss physiognomist Lavater, as
'full of genius, piercing, fascinating, magical', and the
lower part of his face as 'sweet, affable and sociable'. It
could not have been otherwise, for he was a man of great
personal integrity and candour, highly sympathetic,
generous to a fault and rich in feeling. His mistress, Mrs
Armistead, who lived with him for ten years before he
married her in 1795, was devoted to him. She was said to
have been the daughter of a Methodist preacher and to
have grown into such a beautiful young woman, she was

o

soon to be found in a certain notorious establishment in Marlborough Street, which had nothing whatever to do with the Methodists. The Prince of Wales saw her and loved her before he met Mrs Fitzherbert and Reynolds painted her looking her best in a large black hat plumed with gorgeous white feathers. Both Lord George Cavendish and the Earl of Derby enjoyed her favours, but once she had settled with Fox she was faithful to him for life, and clever with him too. She knew exactly how to manage her 'beloved angel' and gave him peace and happiness at their charming country villa at St Anne's Hill near Chertsey, from whence he wrote to his nephew of 'the place looking beautiful beyond all description, the nightingales singing, and Mrs A as happy as the day is long—all of which circumstances combine to enable me to bear public calamities with philosophy'.

It was not so easy for the Prince of Wales to be philosophical. Pitt's delaying tactics and the King's recovery of his wits in 1789 had shelved for the time being the whole idea of a Regency. The Prince had no power in the state, no object to work for and nothing to occupy his leisure except the amusement he got from improving his house in London and the villa he rented at Brighton. Carlton House was remodelled by a rising young architect, Henry Holland, and made into a superb residence. Even Horace Walpole thought highly of it. 'There is an august simplicity which astonished me,' he declared. 'You cannot call it magnificent; it is the taste and the propriety that strike.' And not being an admirer of Adam's later style, he added: 'How sick one shall be after this chaste palace, of Mr Adam's gingerbread and snippets of embroidery.' Not that chastity was ever quite the Prince's aim in his passion for art and architecture, or in his other methods of enjoying himself. He was much too fond of luxury and ease, far too voluptuous to curb his appetite and all too eager to taste what life had to offer. He had no use for his father's

preference for mutton and caper sauce and never diluted
his wine with water. His dinners at Carlton House were
served *à la russe* and lasted some five or six hours with all
the most exotic French dishes his chef could concoct. He
liked hot lobsters, salmon cooked in butter, ducks and
chicken *à la provençale*, rich sauces, mushrooms and
truffles, soufflés piled high with chocolate and cream,
pastries, meringues and syllabubs laced with wine. He was
not very worried when he was young, about the effects on
his liver or his waistline,and the cost of his dinners, as of
his whole establishment, worried him even less. Grocers
and haberdashers, tailors, coach-builders and confec-
tioners were only too happy to give him credit in return
for the honour of serving him and being able to add the
emblem of his feathers 'By Appointment' to the top of their
unpaid bills.

But it was at Brighton that the Prince enjoyed himself
most. Once an obscure little fishing village called Bright-
helmstone, where the coarse black pigs from the down-
land farms came rooting round the muddy little stream
running by the Steine and the lusty boatmen hauled their
nets of silver fish in from the sea, it had been discovered
by a certain Dr Russell in 1750, when the idea of sea-
bathing as a cure for all kinds of sickness had suddenly
become a fashionable craze. Mrs Thrale went there with
her daughters and Fanny Burney, who survived being
dipped in the icy ocean before dawn on a bleak November
morning and apparently benefited from drinking sea-
water mixed with port wine and milk. Others suffering
from melancholia, disorders of the stomach, vertigo and
scrofula did likewise, travelling down from London by
private carriage or by the excellent coach service leaving
the Golden Cross, Charing Cross, very early in the
morning and arriving late at night at the Castle Inn. Here
the accommodation was somewhat cramped and some of
the visitors found themselves obliged to seek alternative

lodgings in the rather dank and smelly cottages of the fishermen. But 'Captain' Wade, the self-appointed master of ceremonies at the Castle, did what he could for their comfort and their entertainment. He had his assemblies two nights a week, card parties, concerts and balls, and he built a new theatre in North Street to attract the more celebrated players down from London. For the ladies' amusement there were the shops and the libraries, and the gentlemen, when they were tired of hunting the ladies, could go and hunt the hare on the downs instead or go to the races at Lewes; and, of course, there was the bathing, though this was more of a penance than a pleasure and consisted of being dipped under the water by 'Old Smoaker' or Martha Gunn, who were practically indistinguishable from each other as to sex, size and complexion, both of them being large and leathery, though the latter wore a tired black bonnet like the witch of Endor and the former a red woollen cap with a tassel.

'Captain' Wade rang the bells when the Prince arrived on his first visit to his uncle Cumberland in 1783 and a royal salute was fired, which unhappily shot one of the gunners into the sea and killed him. But it was after the Prince had selected a house of his own on the west side of the Steine that the one-time fishing village began to expand into the gayest and most fashionable resort in the whole of Europe. Bath had declined in popularity and though amusing enough in 1800 to that wide-eyed, observant young woman Jane Austen, was now, according to the Duchess of Devonshire, 'the most hateful of places for scandalous ill-nature, owing to the swarm of Old Maids, Old Cats and Old Batchelors that live in it.' Brighton was for the young intent on enjoying themselves, with time enough to squander as they chose. Before long the fish-carts and the fishermen, the black pigs and the invalid carriages were outnumbered by the smart equipages of the wealthy young aristocrats, the *nouveaux riches*

and hangers-on of the fast set revolving round the heir
to the throne. The Steine was crowded with curricles,
phaetons, tandems, buggies and barouches drawn by
superbly glossy horses and driven by their owners with
great panache. The pebble cottages lying all hugger-
mugger close to the sea and stinking of fish, were no
longer needed as lodgings, for new houses with bow-
windows and balconies, elegant drawing-rooms and small
front gardens railed in by decorative ironwork were rising
everywhere to improve the appearance of the town and to
welcome the modish visitors.

The Prince's house when he first made it his summer
residence was not much more than a *cottage orné* or a
respectable farmhouse. Over the years it was to become
his pleasure-dome of quasi-oriental magnificence; to
some of his critics his worst and most extravagant folly,
to others with more understanding, the ultimate expression
of his artistic imagination: florid, perhaps, absurdly
fantastic, romantic and theatrical, yet always original and
never dull. But this was to come in the new century; in
the 1780s and the 1790s of the old century, he was quite
content with Henry Holland's alterations and improvements to the Pavilion, for he was happier in Brighton
than he had ever been before or was ever to be again. He
was popular with the ordinary people, and he had more
freedom than in London for riding on the downs to
review his favourite regiment, the 10th Hussars, for
driving his phaeton at a pace in the sparkling seaside air,
for practical jokes and silly pranks with his riotous
friends the Barrymores, Tommy Onslow, Lord George
Hanger and the Lades, an eccentric husband and wife who
were horse mad and hell-bent on riding themselves to
death. At the races—a new course was laid out on the
downs at Brighton to supplement the one at Lewes—he
sat high up on his German wagon with Sir John Lade
beside him, bowed to the company all around him and

talked at his ease with Sir Charles Bunbury, the founder of the Jockey Club, with old Lord Clermont and the Duke of Richmond. The crowd cheered him, and the audience applauded when he came into his box at the theatre; at the balls at the Castle Inn, wearing a pink silk coat ablaze with French paste buttons, he danced and smiled and was gracious to everyone. And besides all this, Mrs Fitzherbert occupied a house on the Steine near enough to the Pavilion to be convenient and far enough away to give the appearance of two totally separate establishments.

At night she was a charming hostess to the Prince's friends at the Pavilion, while he beat time on a dinner-gong to the loud music of his German band and sometimes burst into song. In the daytime she entertained him at home, or sat in the window of her drawing-room to watch the never-ending stream of prancing horses and modish carriages, the Hussars officers and their pretty young misses strolling by, the Duke of Queensberry out to kill, the Duke of Norfolk stout and never sober, Fox and Sheridan arm-in-arm, and even William Pitt with his niece Lady Hester Stanhope. . . . For all the world came to Brighton and while not far away across the Channel the mob was at work with sticks and staves and flaming torches and the streets were running with blood, the cavalcade of leisure and pleasure in England went gaily on. Soon the French aristocrats who had escaped the tumbril and the guillotine, were arriving at Brighton in fishing-boats and wading ashore with a few jewels stuffed into the bosom of their tattered silk coats and dresses. They could not, after the horror they had seen, believe their eyes. The prosperous seaside town was all brightness, sophistication and fun. Was it possible—or were they dreaming?

There was the Prince, guarded by no one except Johnny Townsend, an ex-Bow Street Runner, moving freely among the populace; and on his birthday, to the sound of the joyous bells ringing out, driving with his royal brothers and Mrs Fitzherbert to an open space above the town to watch the local folk boxing and wrestling and running races, and treating them afterwards to gallons of beer and the oxen roasted in a neighbouring field. The Prince and his brothers 'with great affability' actually joined in a high-spirited game of cricket and gave out the prizes when the sports were over. Then in the evening, when the sky darkened over the sea, there was a splendid display of fireworks: girandoles, gerbs and gillocks in brilliant fire and rockets blazing in a thousand stars for the rich and the poor to gape at, for the Prince and his people to enjoy.

The French refugees, their ears still buzzing with raucous shouts of liberty, equality and fraternity, and their minds still paralysed with terror, could only stare and wonder. Was it possible that the beef-eating, fox-hunting English gentry had discovered something that the French nobility had overlooked—a way of sharing their leisure and pleasure with *hoi polloi*? It looked very like it when Brighton was *en fête* at the end of the eighteenth century and the brilliance of the fireworks dissolved into the quiet darkness of the sea. It seemed very like it to the English themselves, for ever boasting of their freedom, before the bewildering and dynamic developments of the new century began to change their way of life out of all recognition.

SELECT BIBLIOGRAPHY

ADAM, Robert and James. *Works in Architecture,* 3 vols.
1778–1779.

ADDISON, William. *English Fairs and Markets.* 1953.

AITKIN, George. *Life of Richard Steele.* 2 vols. 1889.

ANTAL, Frederick. *Hogarth.* 1962.

ASHTON, John. *Social Life in the Reign of Queen Anne.* 1919.

BAYNE-POWELL, Rosamond. *English Country Life in the
18th Century.* 1935.

BLACK, Clementina. *The Linleys of Bath.* 1911.

BOSWELL, James. *Life of Samuel Johnson.* 1791. 2 vols.
(Everyman Edition).

BOSWELL, James. *London Journal. 1762–3.* Ed. Frederick A.
Pottle. 1950.

BRANDER, Michael. *The Hunting Instinct.* 1964.

BRIMLEY-JOHNSON, R. (Editor) *Blue-stocking Letters.* 1926.

BROCKMAN, H. A. N. *The Caliph of Fonthill.* 1956.

BUSSE, John. *Mrs Montagu, Queen of the Blues.* 1928.

CAMPBELL, Colen. *Vitruvius Britannicus.* 2 vols. 1717–1735.

CHANCELLOR, E. Beresford. *Annals of Covent Garden.* 1930.

CHESTERFIELD, Lord. *Letters to His Son.* (Everyman
Edition).

CIBBER, Colley. *An Apology for His Life.* (Everyman
Edition).

CLIFFORD, James L. *Hester Lynch Piozzi* (Mrs Thrale).
1941.

COLERIDGE, Samuel Taylor. *Letters*. 4 vols. Ed. Leslie Griggs. 1959.

DEFOE, Daniel. *Tour Through England and Wales, 1724–1726*. 2 vols. (Everyman Edition).

DELANY, Mrs Mary. *Autobiography and Correspondence*. 6 vols. Ed. Lady Llanover. 1861.

DEVONSHIRE, Georgiana, Duchess of. *Extracts from the Correspondence of Georgiana, Duchess of Devonshire*. Ed. Earl of Bessborough, 1955.

DOBRÉE, Bonamy. *Sarah Churchill*. 1927.

DOBRÉE, Bonamy. *Alexander Pope*. 1951.

DOBSON, Austin. *Horace Walpole, A Memoir*. 1893.

DRINKWATER, John. *Charles James Fox*. 1928.

FFRENCH, Yvonne. *Mrs Siddons*. 1954.

FLEMING, John. *Robert Adam and His Circle*. 1962.

FREEMAN, John. *Oliver Goldsmith*. 1951.

GAY, John. *Letters*. Ed. C. F. Burgess. 1966.

GAY, John. *Trivia*. Ed. W. H. Williams. 1922.

GAYE, Phoebe Fenwick. *John Gay*. 1938.

GORE-BROWNE, Robert. *Anne Oldfield*. 1957.

GRAY, Thomas. *Correspondence*. Ed. P. Toynbee and L. Whibley. 1935.

GREEN, David. *Sarah, Duchess of Marlborough*. 1967.

HALLIDAY, F. E. *Dr Johnson and His World*. 1968.

HALSBAND, Robert. *Life of Lady Mary Wortley Montagu*. 1956.

HAZLITT, William. *Essays*. Ed. Geoffrey Keynes. 1930.

HEMLOW, Joyce. *The History of Fanny Burney*. 1958.

HERVEY, Lord. *Memoirs*. Ed. Romney Sedgwick. 1931.

HUDSON, Derek. *Sir Joshua Reynolds*. 1958.

HUGHES, Anne. *Diary of a Farmer's Wife, 1796–1797*. Ed. Susan Beedell. 1964.

JOHNSON, Samuel. *Works*.

LEES-MILNE, James. *Earls of Creation*. 1962.

LEES-MILNE, James. *The Age of Adam*. 1947.

LETTS, Malcolm. *As the Foreigner Saw Us*. 1935.

LONSDALE, Roger. *Dr Charles Burney.* 1965.

LYBBE POWYS, Caroline. *Diary.* Ed. Emily J. Climenson. 1899.

MARGETSON, Stella. *Journey by Stages.* 1967.

MARSHALL, Dorothy. *English People in the 18th Century.* 1956.

OMAN, Carola. *David Garrick,* 1958.

PLUMB, J. H. *Sir Robert Walpole.* 1956.

PLUMB, J. H. *Men and Places.* 1963.

POPE, Alexander. *Correspondence.* Ed. George Sherburn. 1956.

QUENNELL, Peter. *Alexander Pope.* 1968.

QUENNELL, Peter. *Hogarth's Progress.* 1956.

RHODES, R. Crompton. *Harlequin Sheridan.* 1933.

ROBINSON, Mrs (Perdita). *Memoirs Written by Herself.* (New Edition) 1930.

ROCHE, Sophie von la. *Diary, 1786. Sophie in London.* Trans. Clare Williams. 1933.

SADIE, Stanley. *Handel.* 1962.

SELINCOURT, Ernest de. *Dorothy Wordsworth.* 1933.

SHERIDAN, Betsy. *Journal.* Ed. William le Fanu. 1960.

SITWELL, Edith. *Alexander Pope.* 1930.

SITWELL, Edith. *Bath.* 1932.

SITWELL, Osbert and BARTON, M. *Brighton.* 1935.

SMITHERS, Peter. *Life of Joseph Addison.* 1954.

STEELE, Sir Richard. *The Spectator.* 1711.

STOKES, Hugh. *The Devonshire House Circle.* 1917.

STROUD, Dorothy. *Capability Brown.* 1950.

SWIFT, Jonathan. *Correspondence.* Ed. Harold Williams. 1963.

TREVELYAN, George Macaulay. *English Social History.* Vol 3. 1944.

TURBERVILLE, Prof. A. S. (Editor) *Johnson's England.* 2 vols. 1933.

TURNER, Thomas. *Diary, 1754–1765.* Ed. F. M. T. Lamb. 1925.

UFFENBACH, Z. C. von. *London in 1710*. Trans. W. H. Quarrell. 1934.

VERNEY, Margaret, Lady. (Editor) *Letters from the Mss at Claydon House*. 2 vols. 1930.

WALPOLE, Horace. *Selected Letters*. Ed. William Hadley. (Everyman Edition).

WALPOLE, Horace. *Memoirs and Portraits*. Ed. Matthew Hodgart. 1963.

WARD, Ned. *The London Spy*, 1709.

WATERHOUSE, E. K. *Gainsborough*. 1958.

WHISTLER, Laurence. *Sir John Vanbrugh*. 1938.

WOODFORDE, James. *Diary of a Country Parson, 1758–1802*. Ed. John Beresford. 1935.

WORTLEY MONTAGU, Lady Mary. *The Complete Letters*. Ed. Robert Halsband, 1967.

WRIGHT, Andrew. *Henry Fielding*. 1965.

INDEX

INDEX

© *Cassell & Co. Ltd 1970*

A.L. OLIVIERA MEMORIAL LIBRARY

3 1782 00166 0410

DA 485 .M238 LEE
Margetson, Stella.
Leisure and pleasure in the
  eighteenth century